John Warwick Montgomery is Professor and Acting Chairman of the Division of Church History in Trinity Evangelical Divinity School, Bannockburn, Deerfield, Illinois. He is the author of *The Shape of the Past, A Seventeenth Century View of European Libraries, Crisis in Lutheran Theology*, and *The 'Is God Dead?' Controversy*. He holds the degrees of Ph.D. from the University of Chicago, and the Th.D. from the University of Strasbourg.

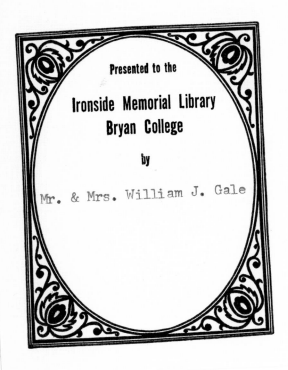

ECUMENICITY, EVANGELICALS, AND ROME

ECUMENICITY, EVANGELICALS, AND ROME

by

JOHN WARWICK MONTGOMERY

Professor and Chairman,
Division of Church History
and History of Christian Thought,
Trinity Evangelical Divinity School

Zondervan Publishing House 🕯Ζ Grand Rapids, Michigan

To
PRESIDENT HARRY L. EVANS
and
DEAN KENNETH S. KANTZER
of
Trinity Evangelical Divinity School
Patrons: et amis

FOREWORD

In this book and in his other writings Dr. Montgomery shows a sweep of knowledge equaled by few theologians today in such diverse theologies as Eastern Orthodox, Roman Catholic, and liberal, radical and evangelical Protestant. This volume presents challenging and acute observations on the ecumenical movement and on current theories of Scriptural inerrancy. Although some of his statements leave my Roman Catholic feathers in temporary disarray, I believe that Dr. Montgomery has fairly presented those positions he opposes. His conclusions are argued so cogently as to demand consideration. This book has much of value and will add a new dimension to the Catholic reader's concept of Protestant thought.

ROBERT CAMPBELL, O. P.
Assistant Professor of Theology
DePaul University, Chicago

INTRODUCTION

Naiveté both of the left and of the right characterizes much ecumenical thinking today. On the one hand, many seem to believe that all changes in doctrine or practice are harbingers of good for a sound union of separated churches; on the other hand, voices are perpetually raised, echoing the venerable cry of "Jesuit regicide," that suggest authoritarian religious conspiracies by Rome or by vast ecumenical units (cf. *Le Vatican contre l'Europe* by Edmond Paris). But change is neither good nor bad per se; each change in the ecclesiastical climate ought to be evaluated without "liberal" or "conservative" prejudice, but with the firm realization that all churches are already one in their participation in a fallen creation. No church and no ecumenical proposal can avoid confessing, as our Lord told His disciples to confess: "When ye shall have done all those things which are commanded you, say, We are unprofitable servants."

The essays in this volume endeavor to point up certain basic failings in contemporary ecumenical thinking and in the theological tendencies currently manifest in Protestant, Roman Catholic, and Orthodox Eastern church life. At the same time, an approach to genuine ecumenicity is offered which avoids these difficulties by taking with utmost seriousness the deposit of faith imparted by our Lord to the original apostolic band and available to subsequent generations of Christendom in the Holy Scriptures. The author's prayer is that this book will aid its readers, whatever their ecclesiastical commitment, to analyze for themselves what must be done to strengthen their own Christian communions and to provide a legitimate and worthy basis for ecumenical discussion, cooperation, and unity.

JOHN WARWICK MONTGOMERY

Strasbourg, France
February 4, 1968:
The Transfiguration of our Lord

ACKNOWLEDGMENTS

The essays contained in this book first appeared in various American and German theological journals. Book publication has afforded the opportunity for slight revisions. Bibliographical data on earlier appearances of the essays in print follows, and the author herewith registers his appreciation to the editors of the periodicals specified:

"Evangelical Unity and Contemporary Ecumenicity": *The Springfielder*, XXX (Autumn, 1965), 8-30 (under the title: "Evangelical Unity in the Light of Contemporary Orthodox Eastern — Roman Catholic — Protestant Ecumenicity"); *The Gordon Review*, IX (Winter, 1966), 69-90 (abridged).

"Sixtus of Siena and Roman Catholic Biblical Scholarship in the Reformation Period": *Archiv für Reformationsgeschichte*, LIV/2 (1963), 214-34 (with German "Zusammenfassung").

"The Approach of New Shape Roman Catholicism to Scriptural Inerrancy: A Case Study for Evangelicals": *Evangelical Theological Society Bulletin*, X (Fall, 1967), 209-25.

"Rome and the 'Death of God'": *Christianity Today*, XII (November 24, 1967), 214-15 (under the title: "Altizer and Rome").

"Hans Küng on Justification": *United Evangelical Action*, XXIV (August, 1965), 28.

"Alonzo Schökel on Holy Scripture": *Eternity*, XVIII (September, 1967), 48-49.

"Archbishop Söderblom's Ecumenicity": *Evangelical Missions Quarterly*, V (Fall, 1968), 53-54.

CONTENTS

Dedication

Foreword — *Robert Campbell, O.P.*

Introduction

Acknowledgments

I

Evangelical Unity and Contemporary Ecumenicity

I

Evangelical Unity and Contemporary Ecumenicity[1]

Apologia pro Dissertatione sua

With deferential bow to the shade of John Henry Cardinal Newman, I must begin this essay in a spirit of personal apologia. Readers of a recent issue of *Newsweek* will have met the present essayist as an apparent ecclesiastical reactionary. Having quoted my judgment that contemporary renewal theology is "so preoccupied with sinful man's needs in our times that it is allowing the gospel to be swallowed up in the sinful situation,"[2] *Newsweek's* religion editor commented:

> None of the "sinful situations" that vex the fundamentalists — whose greatest strength lies in the South and rural Midwest — is spelled out in detail. But their antipathies are well known, particularly toward the mainline churches' involvement in interracial projects, peace conferences, ecumenical dialogues with Roman Catholics, and urban-slum ministries.[3]

Were this a factually accurate criticism, then the Consultation on Evangelical Concerns, in asking me to prepare this paper, would have made a *faux pas* comparable to a wine taster's union choosing a judge with no taste buds.

[1] An invitational paper presented at the Consultation on Evangelical Concerns (Clyde W. Taylor, chairman; Carl F. H. Henry, co-chairman), held in Colorado Spring, Colorado, May 17-20, 1965.

[2] John Warwick Montgomery, "Renewal and Contemporary Theology," *United Evangelical Action*, XXIV (April, 1965), 13 (reprinted in revised form in *Why — In the World?*, ed. Harvey C. Warner [Waco, Texas: Word Books, 1965]).

[3] "Church for Unbelievers?" *Newsweek*, April 26, 1965, p. 62.

15

However, it so happens that (1) I did "spell out in detail" the evangelical objections to so-called renewal theology, namely, Bultmannian and post-Bultmannian de-objectifying of Christian theology and Bishop Robinson's situational relativizing of Christian ethics, and (2) I am personally very much in favor of "peace conferences," "urban-slum ministries," "interracial projects" (having acquired the coveted epithet of "nigger lover" for activities in this area), and, last but by no means least, "ecumenical dialogues." As a confessional Lutheran, I hold to the great ecumenical principle set forth in Article VII of the *Augsburg Confession:*[4]

> It is enough for the true unity of the Christian church that the Gospel be preached in accordance with pure doctrine and the sacraments be administered in keeping with God's Word. It is not necessary that human traditions or rites and ceremonies, instituted by men, should be alike everywhere. It is as Paul says in Eph. 4: 4, 5, "There is one body and one Spirit, just as you were called to the one hope that belongs to your call, one Lord, one faith, one baptism."

Moreover, in company with evangelical scholars of various confessional persuasions, I am presently serving on a theological seminary faculty sponsored by a church body, the Evangelical Free Church of America, which has become known for its truly ecumenical motto, "For believers only, but for all believers."[5] Thus it would be a mistake to assume that the present essay is the work of a theological obscurantist who feels that "all are crazy but me and thee, and sometimes I've suspicions about thee."

But the writer is an "evangelical"; and he does look with grave suspicion on any movements in Christendom that would reduce the effectiveness of evangelical testimony. Here, of course, the term "evangelical" requires immediate definition, for the word is employed in many different ways today. To my way of thinking, "evangelicals" are bound together not by virtue of being mem-

---

[4] Our translation here combines elements of the German and the Latin texts of the *Augustana.* Cf. Willard Dow Allbeck, *Studies in the Lutheran Confessions* (Philadelphia: Muhlenberg Press, 1952), pp. 78-82.

[5] See Arnold Theodore Olson, *Believers Only: An Outline of the History and Principles of the Free Evangelical Movement* (Minneapolis: Free Church Publications, 1964), *passim.*

bers of the same Protestant confessional stream,[6] but by their firm adherence to certain common theological tenets and emphases. These latter would summarize as follows:

(1) Conviction that the Bible alone is God's objectively inerrant revelation to man;[7]

(2) Subscription to the Ecumenical creeds as expressing the Trinitarian heart of biblical religion;

(3) Belief that the Reformation confessions adequately convey the soteriological essence of the scriptural message, namely, salvation by grace alone through faith in the atoning death and resurrection of the God-man Jesus Christ;

(4) Stress upon personal, dynamic, living commitment to Christ and resultant prophetic witness for Him to the unbelieving world; and

(5) A strong eschatological perspective.

Whether a member of a large "inclusivist" church or of a small

[6] I look with a jaundiced eye on endeavors to persuade evangelicals that one particular confessional orientation conveys the "true" nature of evangelicalism; for a recent example of such an argument from the Calvinist standpoint, see Fred H. Klooster, "The Heidelberg Catechism — An Ecumenical Creed?" *Evangelical Theological Society Bulletin,* VIII (Winter, 1965), 23-33. Lutherans, I hasten to add, are not above this sort of thing either; cf. G. H. Gerberding's once popular book, *The Way of Salvation in the Lutheran Church* (Philadelphia: General Council Publication House, 1918).

[7] My good friend Dr. Donald Masters, F.R.S.C., professor of history at Bishop's University, Lennoxville, Quebec, distinguishes "conservative" and "liberal" evangelicals — the former holding to the inerrancy of Scripture, the latter not (*The Rise of Evangelicalism; Lectures Delivered at the Wycliffe College Alumni Meetings in 1960* [Toronto: Evangelical Publishers, 1961]). Though this is a sound distinction *historically,* Professor Masters rightly refuses to give it *normative* status; he is quick to identify himself with those who believe that "faith in the divine inspiration of Scripture is necessary if Evangelicalism is to regain its old power" (p. 15). Moreover I myself have argued *in extenso* elsewhere that a non-inerrancy view of biblical inspiration is both philosophically and theologically "meaningless" (in the strict analytical sense of the term), and therefore constitutes at best an inconsistent evangelicalism; see my article, "Inspiration and Inerrancy: A New Departure," *Evangelical Theological Society Bulletin,* VIII (Spring, 1965), 45-75 (this essay appears in revised form in my book, *Crisis in Lutheran Theology* [2 vols.; Grand Rapids, Mich.: Baker Book House, 1967], I, 15-144).

"separated" body, whether Anglican or Pentecostal, an evangelical regards himself in home territory where the above theological atmosphere exists. Indeed, if we are to be ruthlessly honest, he ordinarily finds more genuine Christian fellowship with evangelicals outside his own church body than with non-evangelicals within it. Why? Because a firm, uncompromising stand on the objective authority of Scripture and the necessity of personal salvation through the subjective acceptance of the Christ of Scripture appeared to the evangelical as the bedrock of Christianity itself.

Evangelicals such as this writer are, therefore, in many ways naturally ecumenical. Conditioned historically by the interconfessional American experience of the frontier revivals,[8] evangelicals in this country have found it very difficult to push other evangelical believers beyond the pale, regardless of the "aberrational" views they may entertain on minor doctrines or the particular denominational affiliations they may hold. The twentieth century has accelerated the tempo of evangelically ecumenical contacts: the communications revolution has brought geographically insulated evangelical denominations into close proximity — and has made Consultations such as this, involving participants from all over America, readily feasible; America's "coming of age" has reduced almost to nil the isolated linguistic-cultural pockets of nineteenth-century evangelical orthodoxy; the growth and organization of American denominations have put evangelicals of various confessional persuasions into each others' back yards from suburbia to the foreign mission field; and the increasing pressures of secularism and unbelief in the mid-twentieth century have acted as a strong incentive to evangelicals to draw closer together for mutual support and more effective witness. The present-day spirit of evangelicalism was well voiced in a 1961 editorial in *Christianity Today* (itself a powerful evidence of the transdenominational perspective of today's evangelical cause); under the rubric, "A Plea for Evangelical Unity," readers were reminded

[8] Cf. Frederick Jackson Turner's epochal "Frontier Thesis" — that the frontier has been the single most important factor in shaping the American character.

in the strongest terms that " 'Be of the same mind one toward another' is the direction of the inerrant and infallible Word." [9]

But while evangelicals have more and more been discovering that — to use English littérateur Charles Williams' moving phrase — "their life and death is with their neighbor," [10] other religious unity movements have been gaining ascendancy in Christendom. Here we refer not primarily to the "objective" amalgamations of Protestant denominations in the twentieth century, but more especially to what H. Paul Douglas has called "those deep undercurrents of Christian unity which are emotionally or mystically realized" [11] — chief of which, in the preceding lustrum, has unquestionably been the ecumenical relations among Orthodox Eastern, Roman Catholic, and Protestant bodies. As Handspicker rightly stated in the conclusion of his recent "Survey of Church Union Negotiations, 1961-1963":

> In the realm of Christian unity "emotionally or mystically realized" we must . . . note the impetus toward Christian concord and unity in two recent developments: the ecumenical impetus given to the Roman Catholic Church through the work of Pope John XXIII, and the increasing and deepening participation of the Orthodox Churches in the work of the World Council. Within the Second Vatican Council the most widely known expressions of this first development have occurred, but of at least equal importance is the attendant phenomenon of increasing dialogue between Roman Catholic, Anglican, Orthodox, and Protestant clergy and laity both in international conferences and in local dioceses and parishes. Increased Orthodox participation in the work of the World Council is not merely in terms of numbers, but in addition through a change in role from "observer and adviser" in ecumenical conferences to fully committed participant.[12]

Faced with this present climate of ever-deepening Orthodox Eastern-Roman Catholic — "mainline" Protestant ecumenical relations, the evangelical churchman finds himself reacting ambivalently. On the one hand, he recognizes with thanksgiving to

[9] *Christianity Today,* March 13, 1961, p. 24.

[10] Cf. Montgomery, *The Shape of the Past* ("History in Christian Perspective," 1; Ann Arbor, Michigan: Edwards Brothers, 1963), pp. 150-151.

[11] H. Paul Douglas, *A Decade of Objective Progress in Church Unity: 1927-1936* (New York: Harper, 1937), p. xiii.

[12] *Ecumenical Review,* XVI (July 1964), 443.

God that the Roman Catholic church and the Orthodox Eastern churches have never ceased to stand uncompromisingly for the Trinitarian core of the Christian faith, as set forth in the Ecumenical creeds;[13] in this regard, the evangelical sees these great churches as a healthy corrective to the unitarianizing of the faith which has occurred in more than a few mainline Protestant bodies under the impact of social-gospel liberalism and current demythologizations of Christianity.[14] On the other hand, even the most unsophisticated evangelical is at least intuitively aware of the gulf that historically separates him from Roman Catholicism and the Eastern churches in respect to the other major elements of evangelical belief: Sola scriptura, sola gratia & sola fide, personal commitment & personal witness (in opposition to the *opus operatum* in all its forms), and a moment-by-moment eschatological orientation. The question of evangelical stance vis-à-vis Protestant dialogue with Roman Catholicism and Eastern Orthodoxy becomes especially acute when we reflect that evangelicals (as this writer is using the term) exist in all mainline Protestant denominations; therefore Protestant movements toward cooperation or unity with Romanism and Orthodoxy can hardly help but alter the perspective of general Protestantism and thus indirectly affect evangelical unity itself.

Thus the overarching question to be posed in this paper: Where is evangelicalism to stand as relations grow closer between World Council Protestantism on the one hand and Eastern Orthodoxy and Roman Catholicism on the other? More concretely, (1) Are evangelicals to encourage or discourage their respective denominations in these ecumenical efforts? (2) Should evangelicals, through the National Association of Evangelicals or by way of independent evangelically-sponsored efforts, carry on their

---

[13] Cf. the value for Protestant ecumenical thinking in such arguments as that of Boris Bobrinskoy, professor of dogmatic theology at the Institute St. Serge, Paris: "The starting (and finishing) point of all healthy ecclesiology seems to me to be the dogma of the Trinity" ("The Continuity of the Church and Orthodoxy," *Ecumenical Review*, XVI [October, 1964], 514).

[14] Resigned Episcopal Bishop James Pike's reservations on the dogma of the Trinity are representative of the latter thinking. See my articles on Pike in the *Sunday School Times* (April 30 and May 7, 1966) and in *Christianity Today* (February 16, 1968).

own dialogue with Roman Catholicism and with the Orthodox Eastern churches? (3) What can be gained for evangelical unity from Orthodox Eastern-Roman Catholic-Protestant ecumenical discussions? Urgent as these questions are, virtually no attempt has been made heretofore to answer them in depth;[15] and I confess that only the overwhelming importance of the subject gives me the temerity to enter this tangled thicket in which objective fact and subjective interest are so closely intertwined. I believe that the questions here posed can be satisfactorily answered — but only against the background of more rigorous thinking on the nature of the present theological situation than is usually met with in ecumenical discussion. If we are prepared for some extended "depth analysis," then we may find that solid answers await us at the end of the path.

The Cruciality of Theological Motif-Research

In matters ecumenical, evangelicals are universally convinced that considerations of truth must precede considerations of union, unity, worship, or fellowship. Granted that among evangelicals there is diversity of viewpoint as to how much doctrinal truth must be agreed to for common action, and as to whether a Christian can legitimately be a member of a body that in practice permits error or unbelief to exist alongside of truth, nevertheless it would be difficult to find any evangelical who would engage in common worship where the essentials of the Gospel (as stated, for example, in I Corinthians 15:1-3) were lacking, or who would enter a church union without clear guarantee that the fundamentals of evangelical belief (as set forth in the preceding section of this essay) would be allowed him. Thus whether a "separationist" or a "non-separationist," the evangelical is perforce committed to a stand on propositional theological truth which appears hopelessly rigid to contemporary secularists and broad-church Protestants alike.

[15] Norman Goodall's article, "Evangelicalism and the Ecumenical Movement" (*Ecumenical Review*, XV [July, 1963], 399-409), though helpful in some ways, suffers acutely from a generalized, broad-church interpretation of evangelicalism and from the author's personal alignment with the World Council criticism of the conservative evangelicalism presupposed in the present essay.

When compared with the "tender-minded" approach of the "ecumaniac" ("churches that commune together stay together," etc.), the evangelical attitude toward doctrinal matters is highly commendatory, for it both takes the Great Commission seriously ("teach them to observe all things whatsoever I have commanded you" — Matt. 28:20) and manifests a properly "tough-minded" appreciation for the law of contradiction.[16] But the evangelical concern with doctrinal differences is not without its dangers — though these are not the ones upon which religious liberals are wont to ring the changes (lack of love, etc.). Trouble arises when, in concentrating on particular doctrinal problems, evangelicals neglect to penetrate behind the surface issues to the basic theological motifs that give the specific doctrines their force. The trouble is not that evangelicals are too occupied with doctrinal truth, but that they are too ready to skim the surface of doctrinal issues! Here we can learn much from Lundensian *Motivforsking* ("motif research"), which is described as follows by one of its foremost practitioners, Anders Nygren:

> The most important task of those engaged in the modern scientific study of religion and theological research is to reach an inner understanding of the different forms of religion in the light of their different fundamental motifs. . . . We must try to see what is the basic idea or the driving power of the religion concerned, or what it is that gives it its character as a whole and communicates to all its parts their special content and colour.[17]

Relatively seldom in interconfessional dialogue do we cut to the level of "the basic idea of the driving power" which gives significance and impact to the particular doctrines under discussion. In consequence, we generally experience bewilderment at the ob-

[16] I find William James' brilliant distinction between the tender-minded and the tough-minded especially applicable to ecumaniacs and evangelicals respectively. Cf. Herbert Feigl, "Logical Empiricism," in Feigl and Sellars (eds.), *Readings in Philosophical Analysis* (New York: Appleton-Century-Crofts, 1949), pp. 3ff.

[17] *Agape and Eros*, trans. Philip S. Watson (Philadelphia: Westminster Press, 1953), p. 35. That I am aware of negative elements in the Lundensian methodology can be seen in my *Chytraeus on Sacrifice* (St. Louis, Missouri: Concordia, 1962), pp. 139-46, and in my essay, "Eros and Agape in the Thought of Giovanni Pico della Mirandola," *Concordia Theological Monthly*, XXXII (December, 1961), 733-46.

EPIST.

tuseness of the other party — and create for ourselves roadblocks which prevent potentially fruitful discussion at depth level.

Consider an example apart from the Orthodox Eastern-Roman Catholic scene — an example which, because of its familiarity, will serve as a paradigm for our later discussion. From the Reformation period to the present, Lutherans and Calvinists have attempted to convince each other that the Verba in the Lord's Supper passages are to be understood literally (Lutheranism) or metaphorically (Calvinism). To an adherent of either position, the exegetical force of his particular interpretation is overwhelming—and neither can comprehend why the other insists upon retaining his obtuse view of the scriptural texts. Now although the Lord's Supper problem does significantly depend upon the exegesis of the Verba, this exegesis fits within a larger context in the case of both Calvinism and Lutheranism. For Lutherans, the Verba must be understood literally, for otherwise a "spiritual" Christ could exist apart from the now eternally-incarnate Christ; for Calvinists, the Verba have to be taken metaphorically and "la vertu secrète et admirable du Saint-Esprit"[18] has to be introduced to raise the believers' spirits on high to commune with the ascended Christ, for otherwise the normal human body of our Lord would be divinized and the "wholly other" character of the eternal God violated. Striking even deeper, we see that the issue really focuses on the question of the "communicatio idiomatum"—whether divine attributes can be communicated to human nature; and the answer to this larger question depends upon the even more basic issue of theological starting-point or motif in the two systems: the incarnation (Lutheranism) or the sovereignty of God (Calvinism). For Lutherans, the incarnation must be unqualified, and the sovereignty of God has to be qualified by it; for Calvinists, God's sovereignty is unqualified, and the incarnation must be viewed in light of it. Thus the particular doctrinal question of the Lord's Supper becomes

[18] The words are Calvin's; see my former professor Francois Wendel's *Calvin: Sources et évolution de sa pensée religieuse* ("Etudes d'histoire et de philosophie religieuses, publiées par la Faculté de Théologie Protestante de l'Universitè de Strasbourg," No. 41; Paris: Presses Universitaires de France, 1950), p. 270. Dean Wendell's book has recently appeared in English translation.

a manifestation of the fundamental motifs of the two theological systems under discussion: Calvinism: with the First Person of the Trinity as its starting-point, and Lutheranism, with its focus on the Second Person of the Trinity.

Once discussion has reached the level of root motifs, the really important questions can be asked. Are the variant motifs *biblical?* (In the case of motifs lying at the center of the great confessional streams of Christendom, the answer will almost always be a qualified "Yes"; in theology as in politics, the devil finds it difficult to fool "all of the people all of the time.") Are the motifs *equally* satisfactory for interpreting the doctrine(s) at issue? (Here the sensitivity of the theologian to the total impact of the scriptural message will be particularly tested.) Can a biblically-grounded calculus be developed to *interrelate* properly the several genuinely scriptural motifs underlying the confessional positions of Christian churches? (For example, the Calvinist "First Person" motif might be establshed as fundamental in the realm of creation, the Lutheran "Second Person" motif as basic in matters of "new creation," i.e., redemption.)

In general, it appears to me that problems of Christian unity, as seen from the evangelical perspective of objective theological truth, require a rigorous "motif-level" examination of confessional orientations — with a view toward the ultimate building of a metatheological calculus for the proper interrelating of those motifs that survive the scriptural test. Such a metatheological calculus would theoretically provide what evangelicals have longed for since the days of Calixtus' commendable but question-begging *consensus quinquesaecularis*:[19] a fully realistic map for Christian cooperation, fellowship, unity — and even organic union.

The development of a metatheological calculus would require the concentrated labors of evangelicalism's most devoted scholars and churchmen; here we can only point to the overwhelming need, both theoretical and practical, for it. Our specific concern at this point is the more modest one of orientating evangelical

---

[19] I am firmly convinced that the ecumenical efforts of Georg Calixtus (1586-1656) have been unjustly maligned; see my Strasbourg University dissertation for the degree of Docteur de l'Université, mention Théologie Protestante: "Cross and Crucible" (3 vols.; 1964), I, 283-86.

thinking to motif issues, so that mature evaluation can be made of Protestant-Orthodox ecumenicity and Roman Catholic resurgence in our time.

The "Geist" of Eastern Orthodoxy

Protestants in general—and perhaps evangelicals in particular—are remarkably vague in their knowledge of the Orthodox Eastern churches. For many Protestants, "Eastern Orthodoxy" is a monolithic entity; whereas in fact it consists of Byzantine, Syrian, Armenian, and Alexandrian (Coptic) traditions, and within the Byzantine tradition alone one must think in terms of Greek, Russian, Serbian, Ukrainian, Bulgarian, Albanian, and Rumanian churches, as well as Arabic-language churches under jurisdiction of the Alexandrian, Antiochan, and Jerusalem patriarchates. If pressed to characterize the history and distinctive position of the Orthodox churches, the most knowledgeable Protestant clergy would perhaps dredge up from seminary days the judgment that in A.D. 1054 the split between the Eastern and Western church took place over the iconoclastic issue and the *filioque* clause in the Nicene Creed"; beyond this, little would ordinarily be ventured other than the common opinion that "Eastern Orthodoxy is practically the same as Roman Catholicism except that the former will not accept the authority of the pope." Upon such fragmentary and superficial knowledge naive opinions are readily voiced concerning Orthodoxy's growing participation in Protestant ecumenical discussions; e.g., "The presence of Orthodox churches in the World Council is tantamount to a Romanizing of Protestantism," or (conversely), "The presence of Orthodoxy in the World Council is to be encouraged as a counterpoise to the exclusivistic historical claims of Rome."

In point of fact, we shall forever remain on the periphery of the Eastern Orthodox question if we do not penetrate beyond superficial generalizations to the heart motifs of Orthodoxy. To focus attention on the year 1054 is like endeavoring to discover the essence of the American character by referring to Columbus' discovery of America in 1492; as historians and specialists in the history of dogma have been at pains to emphasize, the division date 1054 does no more than mark — by way of political conflict and diplomatic ineptitude — a breach which had been widening for centuries and which reflected two distinctive approaches to the Christian faith.[20] The question as to whether the Holy Spirit proceeds from the Father "and from the Son" (*filioque* — in the Western form of the Creed) or from the Father *through* the Son (the Eastern doctrine) parallels the Lord's Supper issue in Lutheranism-Calvinism: it is not a root problem *per se,* but a clear manifestation of a conflict over fundamental motifs. Until we penetrate to this basic motif-level we shall neither be able to rid ourselves of the fallacy that the Orthodox Eastern churches are really "Roman Catholic bodies without a pope," nor be in a position adequately to evaluate Orthodoxy's significance for evangelical unity.

What is the central key that unlocks the exotic treasure house of Orthodox Eastern doctrine? This is by no means an easy question; witness the variation of opinion among Orthodox theologians themselves who have wrestled with the problem! Within the extensive modern literature of Orthodoxy,[21] one finds three especially persuasive interpretations of the *Geist* of the Eastern

[20] See Yves M.-J. Congar, "Neuf cents ans après: Notes sur le 'Schisme oriental,'" and Anton Michel, "Schisma und Kaiserhof im Jahre 1054," both in *1054-1954: L'Eglise et les églises . . . Etudes et travaux sur l'Unité chrétienne offerts à Dom Lambert Beauduin* (2 vols.; Gembloux [Belgium]: Editions de Chevetogne, 1954), I, 3ff., 351ff. In English, see Congar's article, "Ecclesiological Awareness in the East and in the West from the Sixth to Eleventh Century," in *The Unity of the Churches of God,* ed. and trans. Polycarp Sherwood (Baltimore: Helicon, 1963), pp. 161-63; and M.-J. Le Guillou, *The Spirit of Eastern Orthodoxy,* trans. Donald Attwater ("Twentieth Century Encyclopedia of Catholicism," 135; New York: Hawthorn Books, 1962), pp. 90ff.

[21] One of the most helpful guides through this bibliographical thicket has been provided by my good friend and Orthodox believer Ray H. Suput, formerly head librarian of the Garrett Theological Seminary and presently assistant librarian at Western Reserve University: "Eastern Orthodoxy in a Descriptive and Bibliographical Outline," *American Theological Library Association Proceedings,* XVI (1962), 116-35. It will be noted from this bibliography that of the quality literature in western languages, a large proportion is in French; this is explained by the fact that with the closing down of Orthodox seminaries in Russia following the Communist Revolution in 1917, émigrés founded the great Institut St. Serge in Paris, which (together with the more recently established St. Vladimir Seminar in New York and the Holy Cross Greek Orthodox Theological School in Brookline, Mass.) constitutes a focal center for present-day Orthodox theological activity.

church. Professor George Florovsky of Harvard sees the heart of Orthodoxy in its "Christian Hellenism" [22] — in its preservation of the φρόνημα or mind of the Patristic church.[23] Evidently, however, this interpretation is at least in part a *petitio principii* (as Florovsky would of course admit); one must still ask: Of what specifically and uniquely does the "mind" of the Hellenistic Fathers consist? The classic answer was given by the pre-eminent lay theologian A. S. Khomiakov (1804-1860) in his concept *Sobornost*. This term can be regarded as a slavonic equivalent of "catholicity," but not with the Roman connotation of centralized magisterial authority.[24]

> Like the Holy Trinity, multiple in persons but one in substance, it [the Church] unites the living and the dead in a living organism, the "Sobornost," where revealed truth is entrusted to their mutual love; alone among all societies it possesses truth and unity at the same time — outside of it one can have neither the one nor the other.[25]

> Khomiakov had especially developed the idea of a community of all the faithful of one mind (in Russian: *sobornost*). According to him Catholicism possesses unity without liberty; Protestantism, liberty without unity; while Oriental Orthodoxy would realize liberty and unity in love.[26]

> Sobornost is the statement that the Christ-Event has created and placed in the stream of history the event of the Christ-bearing

[22] Florovsky's monumental work setting forth this theme is his *Puti russkago bogoslovija* (Paris, 1937). Interestingly, Florovsky's contention that in New Testament study Hellenistic elements must not be invidiously set against Hebrew characteristics (as Thorlief Boman and the Protestant Neo-Orthodox "biblical theology movement" have done) has received compelling support from philologist James Barr (*The Semantics of Biblical Language* [London: Oxford University Press, 1961]). Cf. my *Shape of the Past (op. cit.* in n. 10), pp. 43, 60.

[23] See Florovsky's article, "The Ethos of the Orthodox Church," *Ecumenical Review*, XII (1960), 189, 192. Cf. Vasil T. Istavridis, "Orthodox and Lesser Eastern Churches," in *Twentieth Century Christianity*, ed. Stephen Neill (London: Collins, 1961), pp. 92-94.

[24] Vitaly Borovoy, "The Meaning of Catholicity," *Ecumenical Review*, XVI (October, 1963), 31-32.

[25] Clément Lialine, "La Position spéciale de l'Orthodoxie dans le problème oecuménique," in *1054-1954: L'Eglise et les églises*, II, 396.

[26] Bernard Schultze, "Latin Theology and Oriental Theology," in *The Unity of the Churches of God*, p. 199.

community. This Christ-bearing community is a free union of
men, brought about by the reception of the Holy Spirit.[27]

Here we see that the *Sobornost* concept points beyond itself to
a kind of mystical relation between earth and heaven, the living
and the dead, and that this organic union is grounded in Trinitarian love and more especially in the Holy Spirit. Thus the contemporary Orthodox theologians Schmemann and Bobrinskoy find
in the divine life of the Trinity the spirit of the Eastern church.
In defense of conciliar (vs. papal) theory, Schmemann writes:
"The Church is indeed a council in the deepest meaning of this
word, because she is primarily the revelation of the Blessed Trinity, of God and of Divine Life as essentially a perfect council."[28]
For Bobrinskoy, "the very structures of the Church reflect the
ineffable τάξις [order] of the trinitarian hierarchy"; and the Eucharistic mystery, being "the sacrament of the New Covenant
between the Holy Trinity and the human race, . . . constitutes
the culminating-point of the whole life of the Church." [29] Particular stress is placed upon the Holy Spirit in connection with
the Eucharist, for not the Verba but the Epiclesis (the invoking
of the Spirit so that the elements "may become the Body of the
Lord and His precious Blood") effects the Eucharistic consecra-
tion.

It is in the Orthodox emphasis upon the divine life of the Trinity and in what my former professor Roger Mehl of Strasbourg
well calls the "seriousness with which Orthodoxy has always considered the doctrine of the Holy Spirit"[30] that we shall find the
fundamental motif of the Eastern churches. This motif can be
summed up in a single word: Mystery. The entire theology and
church life of Eastern Christendom is an effort to give organic
expression to the unfathomable, mysterious life of the Godhead,
particularly as reflected in the Third Person of the Trinity — of
whom it is written, τὸ πνεῦμα ὅπου θέλει πνεῖ (Jn. 3:8).

[27] Charles B. Ashanin, "Eastern Orthodoxy as a Theological Task," *Theology Today*, XVI (January, 1960), 490.
[28] A. Schmemann, "Towards a Theology of Councils," *St. Vladimir's Seminary Quarterly*, VI (1962), 173.
[29] *Ecumenical Review*, XVI, 514-15.
[30] Roger Mehl, "The Ecumenical Situation," *Ecumenical Review*, XVI
(October, 1963), 9.

Space forbids us from drawing connections between the motif of Mystery and all the variegated aspects of Orthodox Eastern belief and practice;[31] a few basic illustrations will have to suffice. *Doctrinally,* we have already had occasion to mention the *filioque* controversy. Why the Eastern resistance to the procession of the Spirit from the Father *and* from the Son — in spite of the powerful biblical testimony in support of the *filioque* position?[32] Because the Western doctrine seems to subordinate the "free," "mysterious" Third Person of the Trinity to the concrete, historically-revealed Second Person; and because the *filioque* appears at the same time to elevate the historical, objective Christ to a status comparable with that of the Father — whom no man has seen and lived — and to give the Spirit, the essence of divine mystery, a place inferior to both. *Architecturally,* what is the almost universal impact of Eastern church construction, as displayed, for example, in such monuments as Hagia Sophia in Constantinople? When that edifice was still new, Procopius of Caesarea (6th Century) wrote of the lofty dome, built so that it appears to have no earthly support: It is "as if suspended by a chain from heaven."[33] A millennium and a half later, the contemporary Roman Catholic historian Christopher Dawson described S. Sophia in like terms:

> When we look at the Byzantine church as a whole, with its polychrome adornment of mosaic and coloured marbles, its antique columns, its carved capitals, oriental in richness and variety, yet Hellenic in proportion and grace, above all the crowning miracle of the dome of Santa Sophia, in which architecture transcends its limitations and becomes impalpable and immaterial as the vault of the sky itself, we must admit that never has man succeeded more

[31] For an excellent treatment along these lines, see Le Guillou, *The Spirit of Eastern Orthodoxy* (*op. cit.* in n. 20).

[32] Scripture calls the Holy Spirit not only the Spirit of the Father (Matt. 10:20) but also the Spirit of the Son (Gal. 5:6); in John 20:22 Christ breathed on His disciples and said, "Receive the Holy Spirit"; and the sending of the Spirit to the New Testament Church is ascribed both to the Father (John 14:16) and to the Son (John 15:26; 16:7, 13-14). The fact that the *filioque* was added to the Niceno-Constantinopolitan Creed by the Synod of Toledo (589) must not be divorced from these biblical considerations.

[33] Quoted in Sir Banister Fletcher, *A History of Architecture on the Comparative Method* (15th ed.; London: B. T. Batsford, 1950), p. 245.

perfectly in moulding matter to become the vehicle and expression of the spirit.[34]

"Heavenly," "transcendent," "impalpable," "immaterial," "spiritual" — these are accurate descriptions both of Eastern church architecture and of the theological motif that infuses it: the motif of Mystery. *Liturgically,* one can enter into the *Geist* of Orthodoxy in virtually any Eastern rite church in the world. The sense of wonder and exaltation, conveyed both by music and text, surpasses even the most elevated moments of the Roman High Mass.[35] One seems almost to be transported into the courts of heaven when, for example, in The Great Entrance of the Armenian Liturgy of the Faithful, the Hagiology is delivered in melismatic solo:

> With angelic order Thou hast filled, O God, Thine Holy Church. Thousands of thousands of archangels stand before Thee and myriads of myriads of angels minister unto Thee, O Lord; yet Thou art well-pleased to accept praises from men in the mystical song: "Holy, holy, holy, Lord of Hosts." [36]

The Belgian Jesuit theologian G. Dejaifve, in an extraordinarily penetrating article, has well captured the contrasting motif character of Eastern and Western theology by the following scheme:[37]

Orthodox Theology	Latin Theology
Mystical	Rational
Negative	Positive
Experiential-existential	Essentialistic
Trinitarian	Christological
Focus on heaven & future	Focus on earth & present

[34] Christopher H. Dawson, *The Making of Europe: An Introduction to the History of European Unity* (London, 1932), p. 120.

[35] I was privileged to study representative Eastern liturgies textually and musicologically under the sensitive direction of Professor H. Grady Davis at Chicago Lutheran Theological Seminary during the summer of 1962.

[36] For the Armenian, with parallel English text, see *The Divine Liturgy* (New York: Delphic Press, 1950).

[37] G. Dejaifve, "Orient et Occident chrétien: deux théologies?" *Nouvelle Revue Théologique,* LXXXII (Janvier, 1960), 3-19. I have altered the author's terminology where the literal English cognates of French terms would mislead the reader.

The Orthodox Eastern churches are *mystical,* "seeing all things in God and God in all things"; the Western church is *rational,* "proceeding from the known to the unknown." Orthodoxy is *negative,* "conscious of God's transcendence vis-à-vis all human intelligence"; the Latin church is *positive,* "establishing itself on what God reveals." Whereas the Eastern church concentrates on *existential experience* of God, the Western church is concerned with the *essentialistic* "how" of the mysteries; it "seeks to explain them." Orthodoxy's "beginning, middle, and end is the mystery of the *Holy Trinity*"; the West's theology is *Christocentric,* "that is, a theology of God made man, 'revealed,' visible." Thus the *heavenly, futuristic* orientation of Eastern theology, as compared with the *earthly, present* perspective of the Western theological mind.

Dejaifve's articulation of the Mystery vs. Revelatory contrast between Eastern and Western theology at motif level leaves us in bewilderment at the accelerating ecumenical dialogue between Orthodoxy on the one hand and Roman Catholicism and Protestantism on the other. With root-level differences so great, how could ecumenical relations be constantly growing closer? Yet such is precisely the case. Roman Catholic journals devoted to Eastern Orthodoxy (e.g., *Irénikon*) are an evidence of the trend; Pope John XXIII's contacts with the East and concern for dialogue with Orthodox Christendom is a matter of record;[38] January, 1964, marked the first time in over five centuries that a Roman pope (Paul VI) met an Orthodox ecumenical patriarch (Athenagoras I of Constantinople) face to face; and the latest issue of the *American Review of Eastern Orthodoxy* informs us that, as a result of the recent Third Pan-Orthodox Conferences at Rhodes, representatives of the Ecumenical Patriarchate of Constantinople met at Rome in February with officials of the Vatican Secretariat for Promoting Christian Unity in order to draft "positive programs for future 'unity talks.' "[39] As for Orthodox-Protestant relations, it is well known that in 1961 the Orthodox churches of Russia,

[38] Cf. Gustave Weigel, *Catholic Theology in Dialogue* (New York: Harper, 1961), pp. 125-26.
[39] *American Review of Eastern Orthodoxy,* XI (March, 1965), 5.

Poland, Bulgaria, and Rumania became members of the World Council of Churches, thus taking a step previously made by the Greek church and by the Ecumenical Patriarch's jurisdiction, the Great church of Constantinople; since that date the Orthodox Eastern theological position has been more and more actively represented in World Council discussions, e.g., at the consultation between Orthodox and non-Orthodox theologians held in connection with the Fourth World Conference on Faith and Order at Montreal in July, 1963. [40]

How different from Reformation times, when in the late sixteenth, early seventeenth century, the herculean efforts of Martin Crusius and the Lutheran theologians at Tübingen to establish ecumenical relations with the East were summarily rejected by Jeremias II, patriarch of Constantinople;[41] and when Patriarch Cyril Lucar of Constantinople, having accepted Calvinist teaching, was hounded unmercifully and eventually martyred![42] Evidently a significant change has occurred or is now occurring in the motif structure of Western theology, Catholic and Protestant, so as to encourage an ecumenical atmosphere hospitable to the mysticism of Orthodoxy. To this new Western theological *Zeitgeist* we now turn our attention.

A New Catholicism and a Neo-Protestantism

The distinguished Orthodox theologian John Meyendorff, professor at St. Vladimir's Seminary, has astutely pinpointed the epistemological gulf that has yawned between the theological motifs of Eastern and Western Christendom:

[40] A brief report of this consultation appears in the *Ecumenical Review,* XVI (October, 1963), 109-11.

[41] See George Elias Zachariades, *Tübingen und Konstantinopel. Martin Crusius und s. Verhandlungen mit d. griech.-orthod. Kirche* (Göttingen: Dieterich, 1941), and cf. Montgomery, "Cross and Crucible" (*op. cit.* in n. 19), I, 105-106.

[42] See George A. Hadjiantoniou, *Protestant Patriarch: The Life of Cyril Lucaris (1572-1638)* (London: Epworth Press, 1961). John Meyendorff, in his essay, "The Significance of the Reformation in the History of Christendom" (*Ecumenical Review,* XVI [January, 1964], 175-76), argues that Lucar really suffered at the hands of a corrupt, "latinizing tendency" in seventeenth century Eastern Orthodoxy; obviously, however, the conflict cut deeper than this, and Meyendorff makes rather too much of an effort to pass over the distinctive motif-contrasts between Orthodoxy and historic Protestantism.

[The] lack, in Orthodox ecclesiology, of a clearly defined, precise, and permanent criterion of Truth besides God himself, Christ, and the Holy Spirit, is certainly one of the major contrasts between Orthodoxy and all classical Western ecclesiologies. In the West, the gradually developed theory of papal infallibility was opposed, after the collapse of the conciliar movement, by the Protestant affirmation of *Sola Scriptura*. The entire Western ecclesiological problem, since the sixteenth century, turned around this opposition of two *criteria*, two references of doctrinal *security*, while in Orthodoxy no need for, or necessity of, such a security was ever really felt, for the simple reason that the living Truth is its own criterion.[43]

As a historical statement, this is precisely accurate: the existential mysticism of the Orthodox Eastern churches has stood in marked contrast to the "rational," "essentialistic" concern of Romanism and Protestantism for objective, external authority. Today, however, in practice if not in theory, the Western theological landscape has taken on a significantly different character.

Prior to the pontificate of John XXIII, Protestant relations with Roman Catholicism could be characterized as negative but clean-cut. The Roman church presented to Protestants a solid wall of Aristotelian-Thomist propositional doctrine (as represented, for example, in Denzinger's *Sources of Catholic Dogma* and Ludwig Ott's *Fundamentals of Catholic Dogma*), and dialogue, when it took place at all, proceeded on the level of objective comparison and contrast of theological tenets held by the respective churches. Common ground lay in the Ecumenical creeds and in mutual acceptance of the propositional inerrancy of Holy Scripture — the latter dogma being held with particular strictness in Roman Catholicism particularly after the papal condemnation of Modernistic biblical scholars such as Loisy at the turn of the present century. Traditional discussions between Romanists and Protestants

[43] John Meyendorff, "The Meaning of Tradition," in *Scripture and Ecumenism: Protestant, Catholic, Orthodox and Jewish*, ed. Leonard J. Swidler ("Duquesne Studies. Theological Series," 3; Pittsburgh: Duquesne University Press, 1965), p. 51 (Meyendorff's italics). Along the same line Professor Panagiotis Bratsiotis of the University of Athens speaks appreciatively of "le pieux agnosticisme des Pères grecs" ("La Signification du dogme dans la théologie orthodoxe," in *1054-1954: L'Eglise et les églises* [*op. cit.* in n. 20], II, 205).

would, if pursued far enough, eventually arrive (as Meyendorff suggests) at the question of religious authority, and it would become clear that for the Catholic, church tradition must serve as interpreter of Scripture, whereas for the Protestant the Bible alone, regarded as perspicuously self-interpreting, stood as final arbiter of all religious questions.

Today the pattern of Protestant-Catholic dialogue has altered much. On the Roman side, a remarkable and all-embracing new philosophy of Catholicism has entered the picture.[44] This "New Shape," largely reflecting post-war theological developments in Germany and France, has infuriated traditional Romanism (especially in Spain), produced tensions at the Second Vatican Council and in American Catholic circles, and been heralded as an ecumenical panacea by many enthusiastic Protestants. On the surface, the latter have a point: New Shape Catholicism is positively concerned with Scripture, with the theological insights of the Protestant Reformers, with the need for personal "incorporation" into Christ, and with the reduction of superstitious, *ex opere operato* piety in the church. On this level, evangelical Protestants have every right — and indeed responsibility — to praise God for the new perspective.

But one must not be afraid to look deeper — to the motif that underlies the New Shape. This is the substitution of a "dynamic," "personalistic" category of doctrinal interpretation for the formalistic, propositional, Aristotelian-Thomistic categories of "efficient causality." So Romano Guardini repeatedly claims that Christianity is neither a metaphysical understanding of the world nor an ethical system, but "participation in the existence of Christ Himself"; Yves Congar stresses "the mystery of the Church" (this is the title of his important work on ecclesiology); Dom Odo Casel and Louis Bouyer regard the Eucharist not from a technical, tran-

[44] For material to follow (though not for the over-all interpretation of it!) I am much indebted to Dr. George Lindbeck of Yale, an official observer at the Second Vatican Council, under whose excellent tutelage I was privileged to study contemporary Roman Catholic theology during the summer of 1961. Cf. with the ensuing discussion, G. C. Berkouwer, *The Second Vatican Council and the New Catholicism*, trans. Lewis B. Smedes (Grand Rapids, Michigan: Eerdmans, 1965), which offers an interpretation intermediate between Lindbeck's and mine.

substantiation viewpoint, but as a *mysterion* — as reflecting a sacramental, supratemporal realm between God in eternity and man
in history; Hans Küng argues that Karl Barth's personalistic view
of the Atonement is entirely consistent with, and ought to be incorporated into, Roman Catholic teaching; and Karl Rahner has
set a view of Revelation as "Christ the new reality" over against
the traditional "propositional" concept of revelatory truth.

It is in fact in its approach to scriptural Revelation that the
Roman Catholic New Shape displays its fundamental motif with
particular clarity. Historically, after the papal condemnation of
the Modernists, biblical liberalism went underground in the
Roman church. For forty years scholars of critical bent limited
themselves to the publication of "harmless" material. But by the
1940's, men sympathetic to critical biblical scholarship had
reached high positions in the church, and the less radical Protestant Neo-Orthodoxy had sufficiently replaced Protestant Modernism to remove an overt threat; a policy change therefore became
feasible.

The papal encyclical, *Divino afflante Spiritu* (1943), was the
herald of the new era. Though it did not explicitly permit a
radical approach to Scripture, it clearly allowed the use of the
formgeschichtliche Methode and made it possible for Roman
Catholic scholars to doubt, for example, that given biblical miracles occurred historically if their doubt stemmed from conviction that the miracles were included as literary devices to illustrate
theological points.[45]   In the wake of *Divino afflante Spiritu* has

[45] Roger Aubert has stated that Catholic exegetes could theoretically on
this basis remain in full fellowship with the church while denying all biblical miracles but the Virgin Birth and the Resurrection. If it is argued that
the encyclical *Humani generis* (1950) seems to restrict the liberty permitted
by *Divino afflante Spiritu*, one need only consider Jesuit Gustave Lambert's
well-received interpretation that *Humani generis* does not function in this
manner (a conclusion likewise reached by Count Begouen, the eminent
French anthropologist — see James M. Connolly, *The Voices of France; a
Survey of Contemporary Theology in France* [New York: Macmillan, 1961],
pp. 189-90), and at the same time observe such recent Roman Catholic biblical scholarship as Myles M. Bourke's paper, "The Literary Genus of Matthew 1-2" (*Catholic Biblical Quarterly*, XXII [1960], 160-75), where in a
manner strongly reminiscent of Loisy, Bourke uses the fact that the infancy
narrative parallels in literary genre a haggadic commentary to dispense with
the historicity of many details of the biblical account. (Cf. also Joseph A.

come Father Raymond E. Brown's catalytic dissertation, *The Sensus Plenior of Sacred Scripture* (published 1955), which argues that the "fuller sense" of the Bible must not be subsumed under the *sensus literalis*; this interest in a "fuller sense" has been recognized to have "affinities with Gerhard von Rad's interest in the successive reinterpretation of the Old Testament *Heilsgeschichte* within the successive oral and written layers of the Old Testament itself, or with Rudolf Bultmann's detection that the Christology implicit in Jesus' mission becomes explicit in the Christological titles attributed to him after Easter." [46] In *sensus plenior* fashion we thus find George Tavard, who has endeavored to blend Scripture and tradition into a single dialectic source of religious knowledge, [47] expressing views that might have come from the fonts of Eastern Orthodoxy:

> The scientific reading of a text may well determine the notional sense conveyed by its words, but it cannot approach the real sense. After science has done its necessary work, the letter still remains to be personally understood and assimilated as spirit. . . . The question of how much of Revelation may be known with certainty through Scripture alone raises a false problem: it assumes that Scripture has a noetic purpose as a source of knowledge, rather than a kerygmatic purpose as the proclamation of a Word from God. . . . If scientific exegesis cannot arrive at some of the Church's doctrines, we should remember that scientific study cannot by itself

Fitzmyer, S.J., "The [Pontifical] Biblical Commission's Instruction on the Historical Truth of the Gospels," *Theological Studies*, XXV [September, 1964], 386-408; and R. A. F. MacKenzie, S.J., "The Problem of Myth and History," in his *Faith and History in the Old Testament* [New York: Macmillan, 1963], pp. 69-81.) How different in approach and tone is this New Shape biblical research from the uncompromising older Catholic scholarship — which even prohibited unauthorized reading of books claiming that the inspiration of Scripture extends only to faith and morals (*Casus Conscientiae, propositi a Card. de Lugo* [2 vols., 6th ed.; Romae: Typographia Pontificia in Instituto Pii IX, 1913], II, 409-12, casus 171 bis)!

[46] James M. Robinson, "Interpretation of Scripture in Biblical Studies Today," in *Ecumenical Dialogue at Harvard: The Roman Catholic-Protestant Colloquium*, eds. Samuel H. Miller and G. Ernest Wright (Cambridge, Mass.: Belknap Press of Harvard University Press, 1964), p. 105.

[47] Father Tavard's *Holy Writ or Holy Church* (New York: Harper, 1959) opposes the objective "Old Shape" Roman Catholic "two source theory," which regards Scripture and tradition as equally valid but *distinct* sources of the church's doctrine.

discern the sense of the Spirit. We should therefore continue this scientific study, with faith and in the light of the analogy of faith, until the Spirit, witnessing interiorly to the heart of the Church, graciously opens new insights into His mystery.[48]

As the "mystical" and the "existentialistic" replace the "rational" and the "noetic" in avant garde Roman Catholic theology, the West draws closer to the East, and the epistemological question — the question of how one distinguishes religious truth from religious error — becomes harder and harder to ask, much less to answer.[49]

Little need be said to show the place of mainline Protestantism in the pattern which has been emerging. We have noted above the close affinities between New Shape Catholic biblical interpretation on the one hand and the Barthian *Heilsgeschichte* and the Bultmannian *Formgeschichte* on the other. Vis-à-vis Eastern Orthodoxy, the Neo-Protestant conceptions of revelation-as-event and revelation-as-existential-experience (as contrasted with historic scriptural propositionalism) have no less significance; John Meyendorff writes:

> The authenticity of Scriptural texts is not necessarily a formal or verbal authenticity. The Word of Life is not a theological encyclopedia which has only to be opened at the right page for the desired information to be found, exhaustively treated. Modern exegesis discovers more and more — as for instance the works of Oscar Cullmann, or Joachim Jeremias, have shown — that essential Christian truths, such as the doctrine of the Sacraments, not treated directly by the inspired authors, are considered by them as self-evident. . . . This makes it quite clear that Scripture, while complete in itself, presupposes Tradition, not as an addition, but as a *milieu* in which it becomes understandable and meaningful. . . . Revelation, in fact, is not a formal dictation of certain formally defined truths to the human mind: Revelation in Jesus Christ is

[48] George Tavard, "The Meaning of Scripture," in *Scripture and Ecumenism* (*op. cit.* in n. 43), pp. 70, 72-73. Interestingly, Tavard relates his position to Calvin's doctrine of the "interior testimony of the Spirit" — a consideration that should perhaps offer Calvinists a sleepless night or two!

[49] See Vernon Grounds' recent analyses of the instability of the Roman Catholic doctrinal and magisterial authority: "Rome's Tempest in Theology," *Christian Heritage*, XXVI (April, 1965), 6-7, 13-15, and "The Ironical Paradox in Catholic Theology," *ibid.*, XXVI (May, 1965), 6-7, 31-32.

a new fellowship between God and man, established once and for all, a participation of man in divine life.[50]

Such an Orthodox statement as this is at the same time an accurate depiction of the current Protestant attitude to Scripture. World Council Protestants at the Montreal Faith and Order Conference in 1963 characteristically spoke not in terms of unqualified Sola Scriptura, but in terms of "Scripture, Tradition, and traditions"; Methodist Robert A. Nelson comments on that "breakthrough" formulation in a manner fully consistent with both Eastern Orthodoxy and New Shape Catholicism:

> A stage has been reached in ecumenical conversation where we have gained some perception of the determinative place occupied by Tradition in the life of the Church, as something upon which we all are dependent and as something which operated from the very beginning of the Church's history even before the New Testament scriptures were written. We have also become more deeply aware of the dialectical relationship between our expressions of the Faith and their embodiment in confessional structures, and the Tradition. . . . What has become very clear is that the link between Tradition and Scripture must always be of a dynamic character.[51]

One of the most amazing — and, to an evangelical, appalling — phenomena in the theological literature of the last few years is the Protestant-Catholic-Orthodox "colloquium" volumes in which Protestants bend over backwards (yet consistently with their dialectic, existential conception of biblical truth) to show that Scripture is either insufficient as a self-interpreting ground for religious truth or that its proper interpretation leads away from Reformation theology to Catholic-Orthodox doctrinal emphases.[52] In

[50] Meyendorff, "The Meaning of Tradition," *op. cit.* (in n. 43), pp. 45-46.

[51] Robert A. Nelson, "Scripture, Tradition, and Traditions: Some Reflections on the Montreal Discussion," *Ecumenical Review*, XVI (January, 1964), 158-59.

[52] We have already cited the most significant of these to appear in 1964 (n. 46) and 1965 (n. 43). In the former, James M. Robinson, one of the leading American advocates of the post-Bultmannian "New Hermeneutic," ties radical Protestant biblical criticism to New Shape Catholic developments, and Krister Stendahl of Harvard hits the "Western interpretation" of Paul's "introspective conscience" — an interpretation that falsely(!) draws Luther and Paul together by stressing the necessity for radical, conscious conversion from conscious sin. In the 1965 Duquesne volume, Albert C.

Protestantism the theological *via dolorosa* from Schleiermacher and Ritschl through Dilthey and Heidegger to Bultmann and the post-Bultmannians — a road hardly softened by the Barthian dialectic interlude — has painlessly led to a devaluation of objective propositional truth, making Protestantism the eager swain of Eastern Orthodoxy and of New Shape Catholicism. Protestant, Orthodox, and Catholic do indeed seem to be converging theologically in our time — but the convergence appears to be taking place, not at a recognizable, articulated, and firmly established juncture, but in a mystic cloud of unknowing.

The Potential Crisis and the Evangelical Responsibility

The world in the mid-twentieth century is in an unbelievable state of tension and insecurity. Global war and perhaps the destruction of all civilized life loom as less and less remote possibilities as Vietnams follow Koreas and the arms race accelerates. Unbelief and rank secularism are on the rise throughout the world, from the Russian block with its ideological atheism to the Western powers with their pragmatic Realpolitik. As more and more effective communications make the globe smaller and smaller, the mutually contradictory religious pluralism of mankind becomes clearer to all, including the non-Christian. Under these circumstances the quest for religious certainty and truth assumes unparalleled importance. The world asks, either in longing or in derision: "Do you Christians have the truth? If you claim to possess it, give us a reason for the faith that is within you!"

At this crucial time, when a decisive, epistemologically sound religious answer is needed, the non-evangelical Christian world refuses the question and instead offers existential, non-noetic un-

Outler and Markus Barth hit the "traditional" Protestant doctrines of Sola Scriptura and biblical inerrancy ("It is unwise in any form whatsoever to speak of the 'absolute authority of the Bible.' For the Bible is in no wise an absolute. . . . It is relative to the Holy Spirit" — M. Barth), and Robert McAfee Brown points out that Karl Barth "delivers us from what can be a very perverse notion of *sola Scriptura* that would assert that we go to the Bible and to the Bible alone, as though in the process we could really bypass tradition. He delivers us from a kind of Biblicism that is content to rest simply with a parroting of the vindication, 'the Bible says . . . , the Bible says . . .'"

derstandings of faith which are unverifiable and meaningless to the seeker. External, objective tests of truth are discounted, and the unbeliever is asked to enter a mystical realm of divine "encounter" where, in spite of obvious differences and contradictions in Christian viewpoint, no concrete means of distinguishing truth from error is provided.[53] Thus is the great missionary challenge of our time abrogated.

Yet is not the "community of faith" — the Church — constantly appealed to as the medium of truth? Does not one find this theme almost continually present in contemporary Eastern Orthodox, New Shape Catholic, and ecumenical Protestant writing? The answer is most definitely "Yes," but this appeal to Mother Church is fraught with the gravest consequences when combined with a vague, relativistic, mystical view of theological truth. For what happens when a corporate body lacking a clear external standard of truth and judgment grows in strength? The political answer in our times has been given by way of the Third Reich: the corporate body strives to become a standard to itself, a law to itself. In a word, it presses forward to the status of a Leviathan, that "mortal god" which Hobbes described so accurately.

And churches are by no means exempt from this ghastly possibility, as Rolf Hochhuth so trenchantly demonstrates in his dramatic account of the effect of Pius XII's Realpolitik on the wholesale slaughter of Jews by the Third Reich.[54] Even if we balk[55] at Hochhuth's precise parallels between Nazi and Papal autocracy, we cannot but see the profound truth in the aphorism of Lord Acton — himself a Catholic — "Power corrupts, and absolute power tends to corrupt absolutely."[56] Vladimir Solovyov, in his last work, *A Short Story of Antichrist,* gave a vivid literary

---

[53] Irrefutable decimations of the analytically meaningless existential-encounter theologies have been provided by Frederick Ferré, in his *Language, Logic and God* (New York: Harper, 1961), pp. 94-104, and by C. B. Martin, in his paper, "A Religious Way of Knowing," contained in *New Essays in Philosophical Theology,* eds. Antony Flew and Alasdair Macintyre (London: SCM Press, 1955), pp. 76-95.

[54] Rolf Hochhuth, *The Deputy,* trans. Richard and Clara Winston, intro. Albert Schweitzer (New York: Grove Press, 1964).

[55] Some, of course, have; see *The Storm over The Deputy,* ed. Eric Bentley (New York: Grove Press, 1964).

[56] Cf. my *Shape of the Past* (op. cit. in n. 10), pp. 76-78.

reason to believe that where objective religious truth no longer stands as a firm criterion, none of the three great branches of Christendom has the holiness to withstand the blandishments of antichristian power.[57] And if a concrete, indisputable historical illustration is demanded, then the most "mystical" of the Christian churches provides it: Eastern Orthodoxy, which over the centuries has conducted its magnificent liturgies while unprophetically succumbing to all manner of Caesaropapism — even to the present-day control of most of its churches by atheistic totalitarianism.

In sum: unless an infallible, inerrant Word stands above the church, judging it and proclaiming grace to it, magisterial authority is the greatest liability the church can have, for it will inevitably become the unprincipled tool and demonic reflection of sinful man. Only an ecumenicity grounded solidly and unqualifiedly in Sola Scriptura can answer the needs of the unbelieving world and the hopes of believing Christians.

So the evangelical mandate becomes clear, and the questions posed at the outset of this essay can now be given specific answers.

1. "Are evangelicals to encourage their respective denominations to participate in current Catholic-Orthodox-Protestant ecumenical activities?" Participation should be encouraged only on levels where the foundation doctrine of Sola Scriptura will not be compromised, since wherever the "formal principle" of the Christian faith is dethroned, every other doctrine — including the "material principle" itself, the Gospel of justification by grace through faith — is in immediate danger of being lost.

2. "Should evangelicals, through the N.A.E. or independently sponsored efforts, carry on their own dialogue with Orthodox Eastern churches and with Rome?" Very definitely — but in a posture of *witness,* as did Melanchthon and the Tübingen theologians of the Reformation era, not in a spirit of vague, tea-and-crumpets good will, which does no one service. But to engage

[57] Solovyov's remarkable tale was recently printed in an abridged version in *Christianity Today,* IX (January 29, 1965), 21-27. Another superlative literary portrait of runaway spiritual power is contained in C. S. Lewis' novel, *That Hideous Strength; a Modern Fairy-Tale for Grown-Ups* (New York: Macmillan, 1947).

in such badly needed dialogue, evangelicals must (as perhaps this paper has indicated) come to know Orthodox Eastern and Roman Catholic theologies much more intimately than is presently the case. Stereotypes and superficiality are the death of any worthy theological dialogue.

3. "What can be gained for evangelical unity from present-day Orthodox Eastern-Roman Catholic-Protestant ecumenical discussions?" Several vitally important insights: (1) in our intra-evangelical unity discussions we must resist every pull toward chimerical union on "mystical," "negative," "existential" bases; we must recognize the absolute necessity of seeking God's objectively revealed will in the inerrant Scriptures whenever we would find the grounds for fellowship of common activity. (2) Having had our baptism in fire as to the necessity of delving to motif level vis-à-vis Romanism and Eastern Orthodoxy, let us make certain that we pursue our own unity discussions at comparable depth — always searching for those elements of what we have called a "metatheological calculus," whereby the wondrous goal of full unity could theoretically be realized. (3) Since, as suggested previously, it is a rare thing for the *Leitmotiv* of a major Christian body to be unqualifiedly antibiblical, let us seek to enhance our evangelical position by *properly* incorporating the motifs of others into our theology and church life—thus endeavoring to declare the "whole counsel of God" in our ecclesiastical pilgrimage. Just as the appearance of sects and cults invariably points up negligence in doctrine or practice on the part of established churches, so the misuse of motifs in one Christian body points to their neglect in others. Thus, for example, the despising of great liturgy, art, and church architecture by evangelicals has driven souls to the Orthodox and the Roman church;[58] we have much to correct here.[59] Moreover, our cavalier attitude to the

[58] This is precisely the history of several of the former German pastors who contributed autobiographical essays to *We Are Now Catholics*, ed. Karl Hardt, trans. Norman C. Reeves (Westminster, Md.: Newman Press, 1959); the drabness and forbidding atmosphere of low-church Protestant worship had much to do with their conversions to Rome.

[59] Every evangelical reader of this essay should begin by studying carefully Bo Giertz's little booklet, *Liturgy and Spiritual Awakening*, trans.

visible church and to church authority has often made the evangelical voice of little account in the great moral issues of the day—the racial persecutions of Jews[60] and of Negroes[61] come at once to mind; here we can profitably seek to imitate the stalwart, united front presented by centrally organized church bodies. Even in the matter of Trinitarian existential mysticism we can learn much, for the evangelical patron saint is too often fourth century Bishop (and Arian heretic!) Eunomius of Cyzicus, who declared, "I know God as well as He knows Himself." We must not become rationalists in Christian guise who forget that in the final analysis God's thoughts are higher than our thoughts, His ways than our ways. The dimension of the Holy must enter more into our evangelical circles, where our church life often parallels a secular club more than a congregation of saints.

But — as a final caveat — we must never forget to ground the existential *unio mystica* in the objective word of Holy Writ.[62] Though the Persons of the Trinity are ontologically equal, God's Revelation does not deign to teach as much of the Spirit as of the Father, nor as much of the Father as of the Son. Indeed, apart from the Word made flesh we would be woefully ignorant of the Father's heart and of the Spirit's procession. Thus our theology, as long as we remain under the Cross, must be at center Christological; and the only reliable picture of the Christ is imparted by the written Word. Hermann Sasse has well located the contemporary "inability to express doctrinal consensus" in "the tragic

C. A. Nelson (Rock Island, Illinois: Augustana Book Concern, 1950), which demonstrates the integral connection (rather than disharmony) between scripturally-grounded liturgy and evangelical conversion experience.

[60] In his Preface to Hochhuth's *The Deputy*, Albert Schweitzer writes that the German Protestants did virtually nothing to stem the Nazi atrocities because they were "unorganized" and "impotent," and that their guilt came "by simply accepting the terrible, inhuman fact of the persecution of the Jews." The Roman church, as a well-organized, supranational power, was at least in a *theoretical* position to bring pressure on the Third Reich.

[61] It is noteworthy that the Roman church and the Protestant Episcopal church have been able most effectively to bring their Southern constituencies into line with Christian desegregation measures.

[62] I have developed this point *in extenso* in my paper, "The Theologian's Craft: A Discussion of Theory Formation and Theory Testing in Theology," published both in the *American Scientific Affiliation Journal* (September, 1966) and in the *Concordia Theological Monthly* (February, 1966).

fact that modern Protestantism has lost . . . the ability to think dogmatically, that is, to think in terms of a trans-subjective truth which is given to us in the revelation of God."[63] May the Lord grant that in our efforts to achieve evangelical unity, in our posture toward the ecumenical movements of our day, and in our witness to a lost world, we evangelicals may hold that revelatory truth so high that none on our account shall miss its unambiguous claims.

[63] Herman Sasse, "Crisis of the Ecumenical Movement," *Christianity Today*, V (April 10, 1961), 6.

II

Sixtus of Siena and Roman Catholic Biblical Scholarship in the Reformation Period

II

Sixtus of Siena and Roman Catholic Biblical Scholarship in the Reformation Period

Introduction

In Protestant thought today, increased attention is being given to problems of Biblical hermeneutics,[1] content, and introduction[2] as a result of the so-called "Biblical theology" movement.[3] At the same time, primary-source research in the life and writings of the chief Protestant reformers, such as Luther,[4] has stimulated grow-

[1] Cf. James D. Wood: *The Interpretation of the Bible: A Historical Introduction* (London, 1958).

[2] The works of H. H. Rowley and C. H. Dodd are representative; see Arnold S. Nash, ed.: *Protestant Thought in the Twentieth Century* (New York, 1951), chaps. 2 and 3, and Norman Sykes: *Sixty Years Since: Some Changes in Theological Thought since 1900 in respect of the Quest of the Historical Jesus* ("Third Montefiore Memorial Lecture"; Southampton, Eng., 1960).

[3] The SCM series, "Studies in Biblical Theology," well indicates the general trend. Note particularly in this series G. Ernest Wright's *The Old Testament against Its Environment* and Floyd V. Filson's *The New Testament against Its Environment*.

[4] Wilhelm Pauck calls the modern Luther-research movement a "veritable Luther-renaissance," and says: "A very important phase of contemporary Protestantism is the deep interest shown by many in the thought of the Reformers"; Introduction to Karl Holl's *The Cultural Significance of the Reformation*, tr. Hertz and Lichtblau (New York, 1959), p. 12. Cf. Philip S. Watson: *Let God Be God! An Interpretation of the Theology of Martin Luther* (London, 1947).

47

ing interest in their approach to the Christian Scriptures.[5] And while these Biblical and historical studies are being pursued, contemporary Protestant-Roman Catholic dialogue is becoming more and more articulate, and is inevitably pointing scholars of both traditions back to the Bible and to its interpretation during the Reformation period.[6]

It is of more than routine interest, however, that whereas Protestants have been very much concerned with the use of the Bible by their own spiritual fathers of the sixteenth century, and have even concerned themselves with medieval Biblical study,[7] they have done little with the Roman Catholic Biblical scholarship of the sixteenth century. The tacit assumption seems to be that aside from an Erasmus or a Ximenes de Cisneros in the realm of textual criticism, Roman Catholic Bible scholars of Reformation times need be dealt with only when they are the subject of attack from Protestant divines. For many contemporary Protestants it is apparently enough to grasp the medieval Roman view of the Bible and the sixteenth-century Protestant approach to the Scriptures; the questionable conclusion is then drawn that Roman Catholic scholars of Luther's day merely echoed medieval Biblical conceptions, and therefore the Roman interpretation of the Bible in the sixteenth century can for all practical purposes be assumed from the approach taken to it by the great medieval theologians and from the attacks leveled against Romanists by the reformers.

The fact is that there are a number of exceedingly important works of Biblical study produced by Roman Catholics in the sixteenth century which, though practically forgotten today (even by many scholars of Roman persuasion), had a wide influence both on Catholic and on Protestant thought, and deserve careful

[5] Cf. Jaroslav Pelikan: *Luther the Expositor: Introduction to the Reformer's Exegetical Writings* ("Luther's Works Companion Volume"; Saint Louis, Mo., 1959); and J. K. S. Reid: *The Authority of Scripture: A Study of the Reformation and Post-Reformation Understanding of the Bible* (London, 1957).

[6] One thinks especially in this connection of Father George H. Tavard's *Holy Writ or Holy Church: The Crisis of the Protestant Reformation* (New York, 1959), and Jaroslav Pelikan's *The Riddle of Roman Catholicism* (New York, 1959).

[7] Cf the interest aroused by Beryl Smalley's *The Study of the Bible in the Middle Ages* (Oxford, 1952).

attention today by students of the Bible, of the Reformation, and of the ecumenical dialogue. One of the most influential of such works is the encyclopedic *Bibliotheca sancta* of Sixtus of Siena.

The Importance of Sixtus and His "Bibliotheca"

Sixtus of Siena has been chosen as the subject of this paper because of his key position in the general history of Biblical scholarship, and his influence on not only Roman Catholic but also Protestant scholars of his own and succeeding generations.

The *Catholic Encyclopedia* classes Sixtus among thirty-five "eminent Thomists" of the sixteenth century (among others are Cajetan, Ignatius of Loyola, St. Charles Borromeo, Peter Canisius),[8] and asserts that he "created the science of introduction to the Sacred Books with his 'Bibliotheca Sancta.'"[9] The Protestant *Schaff-Herzog Encyclopedia* likewise gives him a high place in the history of Biblical study: "By the revival of learning the Christians were made familiar with the results of Jewish investigations which were soon to lead to the enrichment of isagogical science. The interest in the Hebrew language grew into a wider concern for Oriental philology, which had a fertile field in the translations of the Old Testament, soon to become of use in the department of text-criticism. The earliest fruits ripened among the Roman Catholics in the work of a convert from Judaism, Sixtus of Siena (d. 1599 [*sic*, 1569]), the *Bibliotheca sancta*, which distinguished between protocanonical and deuterocanonical writings, and which dealt also with matters of special introduction."[10]

[8] Daniel J. Kennedy [professor of sacramental theology, Catholic University of America]: "Thomism," *Catholic Encyclopedia* (16 vols.; New York, 1907-1914), XIV, 702.

[9] Pierre-François-Felix Mandonnet [rector, University of Fribourg]: "Preachers, Order of," *Catholic Encyclopedia*, XII, 368 G. Virtually the same judgment appears in the article on "Introduction, Biblical" (VIII, 80).

[10] Frants Peder William Buhl [professor of Oriental languages, University of Copenhagen]: "Biblical Introduction: Old Testament," *The New Schaff-Herzog Encyclopedia of Religious Knowledge*, ed. Samuel Macauley Jackson (15 vols. [reprint edition plus 2 supplementary vols.]; Grand Rapids, Mich., 1954-1955), II, 180. Sixtus is given a similar place in the history of New Testament Introduction by Theodor Zahn [professor of New Testament exegesis and introduction, Erlangen University] (II, 181).

The important place held by Sixtus in the sixteenth- and seventeenth-century world of scholarship is evidenced by numerous references to him in the Biblical and theological literature of the time. Thomas Stapleton (1535-1598), professor of theology at Douai and Louvain, who, according to George Tavard, "embodies the spirit of the Counter-Reformation at its purest,"[11] considered Sixtus "the prince of the learned,"[12] and said that he was "the most accurate writer of all on the books of the canon."[13] Sixtus "was unquestionably much esteemed" by Robert Bellarmine (1542-1621),[14] perhaps the greatest Roman Catholic controversialist of the Counter-Reformation, against whom Johann Gerhard directed his *Loci theologici*. "In his introduction to his edition of [Bellarmine's] *Index scriptorum ecclesiasticorum*, Le Bachelet states that, in the first draft of his *De scriptoribus*, Bellarmine was guided by St. Jerome for the first centuries and that thereafter he made use of the *Bibliotheca sancta* of Sixtus of Siena. . . . Sixtus served as Bellarmine's guide in his investigation of many an author. . . . The long article of the fifth *centuria* on the errors contained in the Talmud is taken bodily from the *Bibliotheca sancta*."[15] Philippe Labbe, who produced an extensive supplement to Bellarmine's *De scriptoribus*, relies heavily upon Sixtus.[16] On the liberal Catholic side, Sixtus is no less esteemed. Richard Simon (1638 till 1712), one of the forerunners of modern Bib-

[11] "In English Recusant theology, Stapleton embodies the spirit of the Counter-Reformation at its purest. His positions are extreme. They not only squarely contradict whatever conception has been favoured by the Reformers. They also combat the theological opinions of more moderate Catholics" (Tavard, *op. cit.*, p. 231).

[12] William Crowe: *Elenchus scriptorum in Sacram Scripturam* (Londini, 1672), letter "S."

[13] Thomas Stapleton: *Principiorum fidei doctrinalium relectio scholastica et compendiaria* (2 pts.; Antverpiae, 1596), Bk. 9, final chapter.

[14] E. A. Ryan: *The Historical Scholarship of Saint Bellarmine* ("Université de Louvain. Recueil de travaux publiés par les membres des Conférences d'Histoire et de Philologie," ser. 2, no. 35; Louvain, 1936), p. 178.

[15] *Ibid.*, pp. 100, 101, 115; cf. pp. 97, 208.

[16] Philippe Labbe: *De scriptoribus ecclesiasticis, quos attigit Eminentiss. S. R. E. Card. Robertus Bellarminus, philologica et historica dissertatio* (2 vols.; Parisiis, 1660), II, 970. Labbe cites Sixtus 101 times.

lical criticism,[17] wrote in a letter of November 12, 1684: "It is very rare to see a Jew truly converted to our faith. Nonetheless, I exclude from this criticism Sixtus of Siena, who rendered great service to the Church, both by his writings and by his preaching throughout Italy."[18] In his *Critical History of the Old Testament*, Simon asserts: "The Book of Sixtus of Siena, called *The Holy Library*, is of greater use [than Arias Montano's work in the Antwerp Polyglot Bible, Bellarmine's writings, etc.] for the perfecting of us in the Study of the Holy Scriptures. . . . Altho he understood not throughly the Criticism of the Scripture, we may say there are few works upon this Subject which have so much Sence and Learning as this has; and he declares his Opinion very freely."[19] Louis Elliès Du Pin (1657-1719), who, in spite of being criticized by Simon,[20] was himself in the liberal Catholic tradition and more than once suspected of heresy, said of Sixtus' *Bibliotheca sancta*: "There is great Enquiry, and Learning in this Work; it has been, and may be still, very useful to those that apply themselves to the Study of the Scriptures."[21]

Sixtus was praised and his *Bibliotheca* was continually used not only by Catholics of all parties, but also by Protestant divines representing a wide gamut of theological persuasion. The "moderate Anglican"[22] John Rainolds (1549 till 1607), president of Corpus Christi College, Oxford, and dean of Lincoln, cites

---

[17] Cf. A. Bernus: *Richard Simon et son Histoire critique du Vieux Testament: la critique biblique au siècle de Louis XIV; thèse présentée à la Faculté de théologie de l'Eglise libre du canton de Vaud* (Lausanne, 1889), and Charles Robert Feldstein: "Richard Simon and His Contribution to Old Testament Criticism" (unpublished M. A. thesis, University of Chicago, 1944).

[18] Richard Simon: *Lettres choisies* (Amsterdam, 1700), p. 176; for other references to Sixtus in Simon's correspondence, see pp. 100-101, 132. My thanks to the Newberry Library, Chicago, for permitting me to use this and other volumes in its general and rare-book collections.

[19] Richard Simon: *A Critical History of the Old Testament*, tr. from the French (London, 1682), Bk. 3, p. 124. Access to this work and to several others used in this study was kindly given me by the Department of Special Collections, University of Chicago Library.

[20] Bernus, *op. cit.*, pp. 111-14.

[21] Louis Elliès Du Pin: *A New Ecclesiastical History of the Sixteenth Century*, tr. from the French, II (London, 1706), Bk. 5, p. 98.

[22] Tavard, *op. cit.*, p. 228.

Sixtus some twenty-one times in his *Censura librorum apocryphorum*.[23] Sir Henry Savile (1549-1622), warden of Merton College, Oxford, and provost of Eton, who was responsible for translating sections of the Gospels, the Acts of the Apostles, and the Book of Revelation for the King James Bible,[24] employs Sixtus as one of his authorities in his magnificent eight folio-volume edition of Chrysostom, and there refers to Sixtus as a "most erudite and sagacious critic of the writings of the ancients."[25] Richard Montagu (1577-1641), bishop of Norwich and chaplain to King James I, who crossed theological swords with both Puritans and Romanists, called Sixtus "a man of very great learning and of prodigious reading and industry."[26] Among the Calvinists, we find Isaac Casaubon (1559-1614) admitting that though Sixtus "undertook not the defense of the truth but the defense of everything Rome does," nonetheless "reading his work has taught me that he was a very erudite man";[27] this is not inconsiderable praise from one who was considered, after Scaliger, the most learned man of his time.[28] Another important Calvinist

---

[23] John Rainolds: *Censura librorum apocryphorum Veteris Testamenti, adversum pontificios, inprimis Robertum Bellarminum* (2 vols.; Oppenheim, 1611).

[24] He was also an avid manuscript collector, and is mentioned in W. D. Macray's *Annals of the Bodleian Library* (2d ed.; Oxford, 1890).

[25] John Chrysostom: Τὰ εὑρισκόμενα δι᾽ ἐπιμελείας . . . , ed. Sir Henry Savile (8 vols.; Etonae, 1610-1612), VIII, sec. "Notae," cols. 215-16; cf. also cols. 114, 625-26. The Chrysostom was printed by William Norton, the royal printer, in a private press which Sir Henry erected at his own expense, and the type for it was specially imported by Sir Henry; the edition cost its editor eight thousand pounds. At the present time this *magnum opus* can be most readily consulted as University Microfilms No. 20191 (STC entry 14629).

[26] Richard Montagu: *Analecta ecclesiasticarum exercitationum* (Londini, 1622), p. 184; cf. pp. 178, 179, 188. On p. 179 Montagu couples Sixtus with Erasmus and Baronio; and on p. 178 he refers to Sixtus and Baronio as "viri eruditissimi." It is of interest in this connection that Montagu based his *Analecta* on Baronio's famous *Annales ecclesiastici*.

[27] Isaac Casaubon, *Casauboniana*, ed. J. C. Wolf (Hamburgi, 1710), pp. 26-27.

[28] Casaubon held the position of *garde* of the Bibliothèque royale for a decade. The last four years of his life were spent in England because of the unpopularity of his Protestant views in France; he is buried in Westminster Abbey. On him, see J. E. Sandys: *A History of Classical Scholarship* (3 vols.; Cambridge, 1903-1908), II, 207; and Mark Pattison: *Isaac Casaubon* (London, 1875).

scholar who praised Sixtus' work was Johann Heinrich Hottinger (1620-1667), professor of Oriental languages and Biblical criticism at Heidelberg, and one of the greatest Semitic philologists and Biblical scholars of the seventeenth century; Hottinger says of Sixtus' *Bibliotheca sancta:* "In my opinion, it ought to be preferred to the other like productions of the Catholics because of the wide gamut of writers cited in it and because of its sound judgment in many matters."[29] That Sixtus was known and his work used among Lutherans also is evident from Johann Gerhard's great *Loci theologici*, where Sixtus' *Bibliotheca* is cited or quoted at least five times;[30] and from the remarkable subject index to theological literature entitled *Bibliotheca realis theologica*, prepared by Martin Lipen (1630-1692),[31] where Sixtus' *Bibliotheca* is cited under no less than four subject headings—under "bibliorum commentarii" (Bible commentaries), "Bibliotheca sancta" (Theological bibliography), "Ecclesiastici scriptores" (Ecclesiastical writers), and "Patres ecclesiastici" (Church fathers) — and the hermeneutic portion of the work is cited under still other headings — "Interpretatio Scripturae" (Interpretation of Scripture) and "Scriptura sacra" (Holy Scripture).[32]

[29] Johann Heinrich Hottinger: *Bibliothecarius quadripartitus* (Tiguri, 1664), p. 11. Cf. Hermann Escher, "Der Bibliothecarius Quadripartitus des Joh. Heinrich Hottinger," *Zentralblatt für Bibliothekswesen*, LI (October, 1934), 505-522. Still another Calvinist who employs Sixtus as an authority is the library historian Johannes Lomeier (*De bibliothecis* [2d. ed.; Ultrajecti, 1680], p. 259; see my edition-translation of chapter X of this work, published by the University of California Press, 1962).

[30] Johann Gerhard: *Loci theologici*, ed. Ed. Preuss (9 vols.; Berolini & Lipsiae, 1864-1885), I, 43 (*bis*), 46, 80; VIII, 241.

[31] Lipen studied at Wittenberg, became corrector at Halle 1659, and corrector at Lübeck in 1676. He is called a "learned bibliographer" by James Darling: *Cyclopaedia bibliographica [: authors]* (London, 1854), cols. 1849-50.

[32] Martin Lipen: *Bibliotheca realis theologica* (2 vols. [comprising part of his 6 vol. *Bibliotheca realis universalis*]; Francofurti ad Moenum, 1685), I, 160, 174, 580; II, 105, 444, 744. These subject listings are themselves referred to by cross-references, so that users of Lipen are brought to Sixtus' *Bibliotheca* by many avenues. It is of further interest that Lipen cites four unpublished works by Sixtus under other subject headings (I, 160; II, 112, 570, 683). Theologians were also apprised of Sixtus' work through the bibliography of sixteenth-century ecclesiastical writers drawn up by Aubert Le Mire, first published in 1649, and subsequently included in J. A. Fabricius

Thus it is seen that when both Teissier and Moréri asserted that Sixtus' work was "esteemed not only by the Catholics, but also by the Protestants," they were speaking the precise truth.[32] Sixtus was a sufficiently important figure in the scholarly and theological life of the sixteenth and seventeenth centuries to deserve our attention here. But before discussing his *Bibliotheca* and the approach to the Bible presented therein, it is well to obtain a brief overview of his life.

The Life of Sixtus of Siena[34]

Sixtus (Italian, Sisto)[35] was born at Siena in 1520 of Jewish parents. He was educated in the Jewish faith, and was instructed

standard *Biblotheca ecclesiastica* (Hamburgi, 1718), final numeration, p. 183. That Sixtus' *Bibliotheca sancta* has served later generations of Biblical scholars is evident from Kaulen's *Einleitung in die hl. Schrift* (4th ed.; Freiburg i. Br., 1898), pp. 9ff.

[33] Antoine Teissier: *Les éloges des hommes savans, tirez de l'Histoire de M. de Thou, avec des additions,* II (Leyde, 1715), 338; Louis Moréri: *Le grand dictionnaire historique* (10 vols.; Paris, 1759), IX, Pt. 2, 461. Sixtus is included in such general works of literary criticism as Adrien Baillet's *Jugemens des savans,* II (Paris, 1722), 47-48; Girolamo Tiraboschi's *Storia della letteratura italiana,* VII, Pt. 1 (Firenze, 1809), 393-94; and L. Ginguené's *Histoire littéraire d'Italie,* VII (Paris, 1819), 58-59.

[34] In this section we shall, unless otherwise indicated, rely upon Sixtus' autobiographical statements as they appear in his *Bibliotheca sancta* (Coloniae Agrippinae, 1626), dedicatory epistle to Pius V; p. 378 (autobiographical sketch in Bk. 4, letter "S"); and p. 667 (comments on Catharinus and predestination in Bk. 6, annotation 248 [on Rom. 8:28]). (All references to the *Bibliotheca sancta* in this paper will be to this edition, a copy of which I obtained from the Zentralantiquariat, Leipzig.) Other early sources will also be employed, and will be specified when used. Modern works which give information on Sixtus based upon the earlier sources include: Michaud: *Biographie universelle;* Hoefer: *Nouvelle biographie générale;* Darling: *Cyclopaedia bibliographica; Enciclopedia Cattolica; Die Religion in Geschichte und Gegenwart; Lexikon für Theologie und Kirche;* H. Hurter: *Nomenclator literarius theologiae catholicae* (6 vols., 3d ed.; Innsbruck, 1903-1913), III, 80-84; *Kirchenlexikon,* ed. H. J. Wetzer, *et al.* (13 vols., 2d ed.; Freiburg i. Br., 1882-1903), XI, 384-86 (article by Andreas Schmitt). This last article provides in many ways the most satisfactory modern sketch of Sixtus; however, in the present study we concentrate attention on the early sources.

[35] In some biographical accounts Sixtus is incorrectly given the first name of Francesco. The original source of this error seem to be Moréri, *loc. cit.,* who, in reading the title page of Sixtus' *Bibliotheca,* encountered "BIBLIOTHECA SANCTA, A F. SIXTO SENENSI" and assumed that the "F" stood for "Francisco"; actually, of course, the "F" represented simply "Fratre" (Brother). See Baillet, *op. cit.,* p. 47, editorial n. 1.

in Rabbinic studies. While still very young, and against the wishes of his parents, he became a Christian.[36] He entered the Franciscan order, and studied the Scriptures and theology under the "brilliant, eccentric genius"[37] Ambrosius Catharinus.[38] Catharinus had a powerful influence on Sixtus, and though Sixtus eventually came to criticize some of his teacher's theological views and to consider himself more of an Augustinian-Thomist than Catharinus was, there is little doubt that Catharinus stimulated his pupil both to independence of thought and to revulsion against that variety of independent thinking characteristic of Protestantism.[39]

From age twenty to age thirty (i.e., during the decade of the 1540's) Sixtus gained a considerable reputation as a preacher, teacher, and father confessor throughout Italy. According to his own statement, his preaching was largely of an apologetic character, for he says that in his youthful naiveté he taught Catharinus' views on predestination because they seemed so effective in countering Protestant predestinarian views.[40] Among his peni-

[36] Neither the precise date nor the means of his conversion are known.

[37] "Historians and theologians generally have regarded Catharinus as a brilliant, eccentric genius, who did much good, was frequently accused of teaching false doctrines, yet always kept within the bounds of orthodoxy. Pallavicini and other authorities declare positively that the Council of Trent did not condemn his singular opinions" (Daniel J. Kennedy [professor of sacramental theology, Catholic University of America], "Politi," *Catholic Encyclopedia*, XII, 213). Lancelot Politi (in religion Ambrosius Catharinus) was born at Siena in 1483 (the year of Luther's birth), became a doctor of civil and canon law at sixteen, held a professorship at Siena from 1508 to *ca.* 1513, later joined the Dominicans, and died in 1553. His famous pupils included not only Sixtus, but also Giovanni del Monte, afterwards Pope Julius III. On Catharinus, see Jacob Quetif and Jacob Echard: *Scriptores Ordinis Praedicatorum recensiti*, II, Pt. 1 (Paris, 1721), 144-51.

[38] Quetif and Echard (*ibid.*, p. 206) think that Sixtus studied under Catharinus while the latter was in France (at Toulouse, Lyons, etc.) from 1534 to 1543; but this is only a conjecture.

[39] Cf. M.-M. Gorce: "Sixte de Sienne," *Dictionnaire de théologie catholique*, ed. Vacant, *et al.*, XIV, Pt. 2 (Paris, 1941), 2238. Among Catharinus' pincipal works was his *Apologia pro veritate catholicae et apostolicae fidei ac doctrinae, adversus impia ac valde pestifera Martini Lutheri dogmata* (Florentiae, 1520); it consists of 192 folio pages, is dedicated to Emperor Charles V, and was reissued in Germany in 1521.

[40] Only two of Sixtus' sermons have apparently survived. They appear in a collected edition of Italian sermons which I have not been able to see:

tents was one whose penitence may be seriously questioned, and
who did his reputation no good from a strictly religious standpoint: Pietro Aretino, *flagellum principum,* who well represents
the individualistic tendencies of the Italian High Renaissance.[41]

About 1550 Sixtus was put under interdict for having em-
braced erroneous views (probably of a Judaic character).[42] He
abjured his errors and was restored, but soon afterwards fell again.
The consequence was immediate arrest as a relapsed person. He
was imprisoned at Rome, judged by the Holy Office, and condemned to perish at the stake. At this crucial juncture a powerful influence entered his life in the person of Michele Ghislieri,
the future Pius V, who had been appointed commissary-general
of the Roman Inquisition[43] in 1551. Although Ghislieri was
making every effort to stamp out Jewish ideas in Italy, and even
though his general treatment of Jews deserves the most severe

Prediche di diversi illustri Teologi, raccolte da Tommaso Porcacchi (Venezia:
Giorgio Cavalli, 1566), Pt. 1 (no more published). This volume is described
in such fullness by Fontanini and Zeno that it cannot be regarded as a
bibliographical ghost; see Giusto Fontanini and Apostolo Zeno: *Bibloteca
dell' eloquenza italiana,* I (Venezia, 1753), 144. (I am indebted to Chris-
tine Reb, head, Reference Department, University of Chicago Library, for
this citation.) The Porcacchi volume is also mentioned by Tiraboschi,
loc. cit.

[41] "In spite of the strain of religiosity in Pietro's character, it is hard to
raise any very strong objections to the epitaph falsely supposed to have
stood on his tomb,— 'Here lies Pietro Aretino, who spoke evil of everyone
except God. He never spoke evil of God simply because he never knew
him'"; Paul Van Dyke: *Renascence Portraits* (New York, 1905), p. 35. An
exchange of letters between Sixtus and Aretino in October, 1546, may be
consulted with profit: Sixtus' letter appears in *Lettere scritte a Pietro Aretino,* II, Pt. 2 ("Scelta di curiosità letterarie inedite o rare dal secolo XIII
al XVII," No. 132:4; Bologna, 1875), 107-110; Aretino's letter is printed
in his *Quarto libro delle lettere* (Parigi, 1609), leaves 56 verso — 57 recto;
cf. *Il secondo libro de le lettere* (Parigi, 1609), leaf 271 verso.

[42] The suggestion made by some that Sixtus' heretical opinions were of
a Protestant nature seems highly improbable in light of the opposition to
Protestantism expressed by his teacher Catharinus, and in light of Sixtus'
own attempt through his preaching to counter Protestant views. As to the
motive behind his fall, most writers hypothesize, as does A. Touron, "a
secret pride, perhaps nourished by the acclaim and plaudits of men"; *Histoire des hommes illustres de l'Ordre de Saint Dominique,* IV (Paris, 1747),
289.

[43] Not general of the Dominicans, as alleged by Du Pin, Moréri, *et al.*

criticism,[44] nevertheless he was honestly concerned for their personal salvation.[45] "Day by day did he visit the prisons, seeking by every means of argument and persuasion to win the accused from their errors to the obedience of Christ."[46] Among those visited was Sixtus, who, after much persuasive effort on Ghislieri's part, renounced his heresy. Thereupon Ghislieri obtained from Pope Julius III a revocation of the death sentence against Sixtus, and permission for him to enter Ghislieri's own order, the Dominicans.[47] The precise date of Sixtus' entrance into the Dominican order is not known, but it must have occurred before the death of Julius III in 1555.

By the time Paul IV succeeded Julius III on the papal throne, Sixtus had so well reinstated himself in the Church's favor that he was appointed by the pope to preach to the Jews in the Papal States.[48] His success was considerable.[49] Paul became more and

[44] In one of the most favorable articles dealing with Pius V in the English language, the writer says that upon attaining the pontificate, Ghislieri "banished all Jews from every part of the territories of the Church, except Rome and Ancona, where their presence was necessary for keeping up the commerce of the Levant; but here, as a security against their evil influence, they were confined to a separate quarter of the city, and compelled to wear a distinctive dress, by which, should they leave it, they would be immediately recognized" ("S. Pius V., the Father of Christendom," Dublin Review, n. s. VII [October, 1866], 290). In a bull of February 26, 1569, Pius V stated specifically that the Jews were engaged in "divination, conjuring, magic arts, and witchcraft"; Bullarium diplomatum et privilegiorum Summorum Romanorum Pontificum, VII (Neapoli, 1882), 740.

[45] Ludwig, Freiherr von Pastor: The History of the Popes, ed. R. F. Kerr, XVII (London, 1929), 340.

[46] "S. Pius V.," Dublin Review, n. s VII, 280.

[47] Sixtus informs us of this in a touching passage in the unpaged dedicatory epistle to Ghislieri (then Pius V), at the outset of the Bibliotheca sancta. The facts are confirmed in two early biographies of Ghislieri: Antonio de Fuenmayor: Vida y hechos de Pio V. Pontifice Romano, . . . con algunos notables successos de la Christiandad del tiempo de su Pontificado (Madrid, 1595), Bk. 1; and Giovanni Antonio Gabuzio (Gabutius): De vita et rebus gestis Pii V., Pont. Max., libri sex (Romae, 1605), Bk. 1, chap. 3. (For a critical evaluation of these biographies, see Pastor, op. cit., pp. 423-24.)

[48] Cf. H. Graetz: History of the Jews, tr. from the German, IV (Philadelphia, 1894), 581.

[49] Manuscript evidence is cited by Pastor, op. cit., XIV (London, 1924), 274. Sixtus' zeal in preaching to his fellow Jews will not seem strange if we consider it in the light of William James' typology of the "once-born" vs. "twice-born" religionist (Varieties of Religious Experience).

more concerned with the Jewish problem as his pontificate drew
to a close, and his efforts were especially directed against the Talmud. In 1559, the pope and the Roman Inquisition confirmed
earlier decrees ordering the Talmud to be burned,[50] but found
themselves temporarily at a loss to deal with the situation in Cremona: "At this time a large school and an asylum for the perse-
cuted Talmud arose in Cremona, a town of northern Italy, belonging to Milan. A Talmudist, Joseph Ottolenghi, from Germany, opened a school under the protection of the governor of
Milan, teaching the Talmud and having rabbinical works printed.
Every owner of a copy of the Talmud sent it secretly to Cremona,
and thus very many were collected there, and thence exported to
Germany, Poland, and the East. This scanty religious freedom
the Jews retained also under the Spaniards, who were compelled
to carry on war with Paul IV. After the pope had been obliged
to submit to a disgraceful peace, he planned to have the Jewish
writings in Cremona burnt."[51] By this time Ghislieri had become both a cardinal and the grand inquisitor of the Roman
Church,[52] and he placed the responsibility for clearing up the
Cremona situation in Sixtus' hands. Sixtus' knowledge of and
revulsion against the Talmud is patent in his *Bibliotheca*;[53] as a
result of his efforts, ten to twelve thousand Jewish books were
confiscated and burned.[54] However, Sixtus' hatred for the Tal-

[50] Sixtus of Siena: *Bibliotheca sancta*, p. 149 (dealing with traditions and
the Talmud in Bk. 2).

[51] Graetz, *op. cit.*, p. 582.

[52] He received the cardinal's hat on March 15, 1557, and became supreme
inquisitor on December 14, 1558 (Pastor, *op. cit.*, XVII, 49).

[53] Sixtus of Siena: *Bibliotheca sancta*, pp. 149-55, where he not only
summarizes the contents of the Talmud, but also lists representative Tal-
mudic errors under six heads: "Against Christ our God"; "Against the
Grandeur of the Divine Majesty"; "Against the Saints of the Old Testament"; "Against the Law of Moses"; "Against Charity and Humanity"; and
"Other Heresies and Superstitions."

[54] *Ibid.*, pp. 149, 382; cf. Graetz, *op. cit.*, p. 583. Many of these books
were duplicates, of course, since the printing offices in Cremona were a
principal target of attack. It is worth emphasizing, moreover, that "Sixtus
did not have much confidence in the efficacy of the measure which ordered
the burning of the Jewish books. He points to the fact that copies of the
condemned works abound in Asia, Africa, Greece, and even in Germany
whence it will be an easy matter to reintroduce them into Italy" (Ryan,
op. cit., p. 33, n. 2).

mud because of its "blasphemies" did not extend to Jewish literature in general, and he tells us that he was able to save at least
two thousand cabalistic books (particularly the Zohar) which the
Spanish soldiers would otherwise have destroyed.[55]

In 1566, Ghislieri was elected pope (Pius V). That same year
Sixtus' scholarship[56] bore fruit in the publication of the first edition of his Bibliotheca sancta; it was natural that he should dedi-
cate the book to his spiritual father and protector.[57] Sixtus' last
days[58] were spent in the monastery of S. Maria di Castello at
Genoa. Apparently it was his great labors and austerity that
brought on a premature death; he passed away in 1569[59] at the
age of forty-nine. One of his last acts was to burn a considerable
number of works which he had written but which he did not
consider ready for publication.[60]

[55] Sixtus of Siena: Bibliotheca sancta, p. 393; again, many of the books
were undoubtedly duplicates, for Sixtus says explicitly that they came from
a printing office. On pp. 391-93 Sixtus provides a catalog of Jewish works
which he considers valuable for Christian Biblical interpretation. Cf. Graetz,
op. cit., pp. 583-84.

[56] The theological bibliographer Antonio Possevino asserts that Sixtus
possessed an exact knowledge of Latin, Greek, and Hebrew; Apparatus sacer
(2 vols.; Coloniae Agrippinae, 1608). Casaubon (loc. cit.) criticizes Sixtus'
knowledge of Greek, but it must be remembered that Greek was a specialty
of Casaubon, who was one of the greatest classical scholars of the seventeenth century. The statement made by Moréri (loc. cit.) and repeated by
the editor of Baillet's Jugemens (loc cit.) that Sixtus "knew Latin in a medi-
ocre way and Greek hardly at all" cannot be supported by an honest reading of Sixtus' Bibliotheca sancta.

[57] The Bibliotheca sancta was published in numerous editions; the more
prominent are: Venice, 1566; Frankfurt, 1575; Cologne, 1576; Cologne,
1586; Lyons, 1591; Paris, 1610; Cologne, 1626; Naples, 1742 (ed. P. Mi-
lante, who supplies biographical data on Sixtus and lists ecclesiastical authors whom Sixtus omitted from the bibliographical sections of his book).
The hermeneutic portion (Bk. 3) of the Bibliotheca was twice published
separately under the title Ars interpretandi Sacras Scripturas absolutissima
(Cologne, 1577 and 1588).

[58] These concluding biographical details are of course not supplied by
Sixtus himself, for his Bibliotheca was published in 1566. See Quetif and
Echard, op. cit., p. 207, and Touron, op. cit., p. 292.

[59] Not 1599 as stated in some biographical articles.

[60] Sixtus gives a catalog of his works in his Bibliotheca, p. 378, and the
editor of the Cologne, 1626, edition (John Hay) adds the marginal note:
"To date I have seen none of all the works of Sixtus except his Bibliotheca
sancta." Lipen (see above, n. 32) gives imprints for four works by Sixtus
besides the Bibliotheca, but since these imprints are the same as those of

The Bibliotheca Sancta

General Description. Although this paper concentrates on the hermeneutic section of Sixtus' *Bibliotheca,* it is desirable at this point to obtain a general idea of the contents of the entire work. In this way it will be possible not only to set the hermeneutic material in wider context, but also to see more clearly why the *Bibliotheca* quickly became a standard work of reference for Catholics and Protestants in the age of the Counter-Reformation. Here one can do no better than to make use of the quaint and precise description given by Du Pin: "This Work is divided into Eight Books. In the First he treats of the Division and Authority of the Holy Books. He there gives an Account of the Calculations and different Partitions of the Scriptures. He shews what is the Subject of every Book, examines who is the Author, what its Authority was formerly, and what it is now. He distinguishes the Books of the Bible into *Proto-Canonical,* which have always been owned as such; and *Deutero-Canonical,* which were not formerly received as Canonical, either by the Jews or by all Christian Churches, though they were afterwards put into the Canon by Christians; and *Apocryphal,* which were never received into the Canon, though some have been inserted into the Body of some Bibles. The Second Book is an Historical and Alphabetical Dictionary of Writers, Books and Writings mentioned in the Bible, or that have a relation thereto. . . . The Third is of the Art of Explaining the Holy Scriptures. He there treats of the several Senses of the Holy Books, and the different sorts of Commentaries upon the Bible. He unravels the Mysteries of the *Cabbala;* he

editions of the *Bibliotheca,* it is practically certain that Lipen is in error. The titles of all of Sixtus' unpublished works indicate his single-minded concern for Biblical studies: "The Use of Bible Concordances"; "Three Books of Astronomical, Geographical, and Natural-Philosophy Questions Related to Various Bible Passages"; "A Harmony of Proverbs, Ecclesiastes, Wisdom, and Ecclesiasticus"; "A Scholastic Epitome of Romans"; "Scholastic Questions on Romans." His unpublished sermons also evidence his Biblical orientation, for they are all expository in nature: "Four Courses of Lenten Sermons on the Gospel, Preached at Genoa"; "Six Courses of Advent and Pentecost Sermons on the Gospels, Preached at Genoa"; "Eight Sermons on the Six Days of Creation and the First Sabbath"; "Six Sermons on the First Three Chapters of Job"; "Six Sermons on Psalm One"; "Twenty Sermons on the Fifty-first Psalm, Preached at Genoa."

invents a great many Methods of Writing upon the Scriptures, and gives each of them their particular Names; . . . of which he gives an universal Table at the end. The Fourth is an Alphabetical Dictionary of all the Authors who have written upon the Scriptures, and of their Works. This Part is, as will easily be imagined, very considerable. The Number of Authors is very great, and he speaks of every one of them with sufficient Exactness. He ranges them all in different Classes. The Fifth Book is a Collection of Notes upon several Passages of all the Books in the Old Testament; in which he produces the Explications and Sentiments of the Fathers on all those Passages. The Sixth is a Work of the same Nature upon the Books of the New Testament. These Two Books may be looked upon as a sort of Commentary upon all the Bible. The Seventh and Eighth are against those that have struck at the Authority of the Books of the Old and New Testament. He mentions all the ancient and modern Hereticks that have rejected or opposed the Books of the Holy Scripture: He refutes their Errors; and then proposes the Objections which they have raised, or were able to raise against those Books; and Answers them all at large."[61]

This comprehensive encyclopedia of Biblical scholarship inevitably found wide acceptance in a period when Scriptural study was occupying the best minds. Its bio-bibliographical sections alone, though they necessarily suffer from incompleteness and occasional error,[62] made the work indispensable. Even those who disagreed strongly with the author's theological presuppositions found that his *Bibliotheca* could not be overlooked in scholarly investigations.

What does a perusal of Sixtus' material on Biblical introduction say concerning his general approach to the Scriptures? It

[61] Du Pin, *loc cit.*

[62] A list of twenty-four corrigenda is given by Ambrogio di Altamura: *Bibliothecae Dominicanae accuratis collectionibus . . . incrementum* (Romae, 1677), pp. 338-40; and Cardinal Cesare Baronio criticizes Sixtus at three points in his great *Annales ecclesiastici* (38 vols.; Lucae, 1738-1759), III, 38; IV, 358; XVII, 331-32. Possevino, who uses materials provided by Sixtus for the preparation of his theological bibliography (*op. cit.*) finds considerable fault with Sixtus' *Bibliotheca;* however, it is significant that Hottinger (*loc. cit.*) states explicitly that Sixtus' work is to be preferred to that of Possevino.

indicates an attitude of mind similar to that of his master Catharinus: independence of thought, but an independence which exercises itself only within the framework of the Roman tradition. One finds, for example, that Sixtus, over against St. Thomas Aquinas, believed the Psalms to be of multiple authorship; in this "liberal" viewpoint, however, he did not pass beyond the bounds of Roman orthodoxy, for Nicolas of Lyra and Cajetan held the same view, and the Council of Trent by no means restricted Catholic scholars to a single-authorship position.[63] In line with Sixtus' "twice-born," convert character, it is not strange that his exercise of Renaissance independence is more frequently directed to the extreme right than to the extreme left. Richard Simon criticizes him for arguing that one should not make or use new (i.e., contemporary) translations of the Bible because to do so only breeds confusion, and that one should rely on the Vulgate tradition of the Church rather than upon the original Hebrew because there are many difficulties in the Hebrew which even the most learned interpreters have not been able to clear up; as Simon asserts, even Trent did not take away the right of the Catholic scholar to work from the original texts or even to gain benefits from the translations of heretics.[64] Moreover, Sixtus hazards the opinion, which Movers and Haneberg asserted in the nineteenth century and which was condemned by the Vatican Council, that the Church by giving approbation to a merely human writing could by that approval alone make it inspired

[63] The Council of Trent, Session IV (April 8, 1546) included among the canonical writings the "Psalterium Davidicum 150 Psalmorum," but by employing this title it did not intend to specify rigorously either the number of psalms or their authorship; cf. Pallavicino: *Istoria del Concilio di Trento* (Naples, 1853), I, 376. In the Replies of the Biblical Commission (May 1, 1910), a negative answer is given to the question: "Whether the designations *Psalms of David, Hymns of David, Davidian Psalter*, used in the ancient collections and in the Councils themselves to designate the Book of 150 psalms of the Old Testament, just as also the opinion of many Fathers and Doctors who held that absolutely all the psalms of the Psalter are to be ascribed to David alone, have such force that David ought to be held as the only author of the entire Psalter?"; Denzinger: *The Sources of Catholic Dogma*, tr. R. J. Deferrari (St. Louis, Mo., 1957), par. 2129.

[64] Simon: *A Critical History of the Old Testament*, Bk. 3, pp. 125-26.

Scripture.[65] Ryan is quite right to say that Sixtus played an important part in the "revival of ecclesiastical learning" in the sixteenth century;[66] but it is essential that strong emphasis be placed on the word "ecclesiastical" in this phrase.

The Section "Ars Interpretandi." Probably the most widely influential portion of Sixtus' *Bibliotheca sancta* was Bk. 3, dealing with Biblical hermeneutics.[67] An attempt will now be made to see what interpretative approach to the Scriptures was advocated by Sixtus as a leading Biblical scholar of the Counter-Reformation period. Then, with his scheme in mind, it will be possible to compare his methods with those of his medieval predecessors and of his Protestant contemporaries.

Sixtus treats the hermeneutic task under three main heads: definitional, inventional, and methodical interpretation. The meanings of these terms, and the more important divisions and subdivisions associated with them can perhaps best be seen by the following chart, which is based largely upon the summary diagram presented by Sixtus himself.[68]

DEFINITIONAL

(determines the possible senses and interpretations of Scripture)

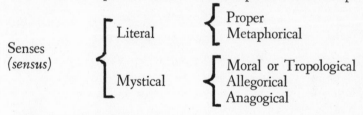

Senses
(*sensus*)
Literal — Proper / Metaphorical
Mystical — Moral or Tropological / Allegorical / Anagogical

[65] Vatican Council, Session III (April 24, 1870), chap. 2 (Denzinger, par. 1787).

[66] Ryan, *op. cit.*, p. 102; cf. p. 178.

[67] We have already seen (n. 57 above) that it was the only section of the work to be reprinted separately. Strange to say, it receives no mention in Milton S. Terry's standard *Biblical Hermeneutics* or in Thomas Hartwell Horne's bibliographically detailed *Introduction to the Critical Study and Knowledge of the Holy Scriptures*.

[68] *Bibliotheca sancta*, pp. 230-31. Not all of Sixtus' subdivisions are included in the chart given above, but enough detail is provided so that the reader can grasp Sixtus' general hermeneutic approach.

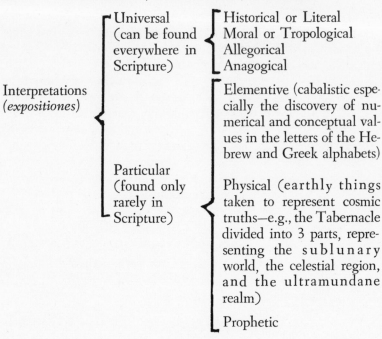

Interpretations (*expositiones*)

Universal (can be found everywhere in Scripture)
- Historical or Literal
- Moral or Tropological
- Allegorical
- Anagogical

Particular (found only rarely in Scripture)
- Elementive (cabalistic especially the discovery of numerical and conceptual values in the letters of the Hebrew and Greek alphabets)
- Physical (earthly things taken to represent cosmic truths—e.g., the Tabernacle divided into 3 parts, representing the sublunary world, the celestial region, and the ultramundane realm)
- Prophetic

INVENTIONAL

(shows what to look for in order to discover the senses and interpretations of Scripture enumerated above)

Literary (studies tropes and figurative expressions)
Topographic (studies the place element in Scripture)
Chronological (studies the time element in Scripture)
Physical (studies the Bible from the standpoint of natural science)
Mathematical (studies the quadrivial elements in the Bible — the arithmetic, geometric, astronomical, and musical elements)
Ethical (studies the moral truths of the Bible)

METHODICAL

(gives in a systematic way the techniques for proper Scriptural "invention" and the presentation of the results of such invention)
1. Translational (use of versions and especially polyglot Bibles)
2. Stigmatic (use of Hebrew vowel points)

3. Verbal (use of concordances to make word studies)
4. Partitive (determination and use of chapter and verse divisions)
5. Epitomal (use of summaries)
6. Eclogal (use of excerpts, and the gathering of them into commonplace books [loci communes] and harmonies)
7. Notarial (use of marginal symbols in one's Bible to indicate subjects)
8. Paraphrastic (use of paraphrases)
9. Lexical (use of dictionaries and lexica)
10. Annotative (use of glosses)
11. Commentative (use of commentaries)
12. Skiagraphic (use of pictures and illustrations — e.g., the Aaronic vestments)
13. Tabular (use of charts and tables for organizing material)
14. Narrative (use of homilies and sermons)
15. Collational (use of dialogue-Socratic form to bring out Scriptural meaning)
16. Meditative (the devotional reading of Scripture)
17. Poetic (use of poetic technique — cf. Boethius' *Consolation of Philosophy*)
18. Epistolary (use of the letter-form to explain Scripture, as Jerome did)
19. Problematical (use of problem-solving approach)
20. Climactic (use of several interpretations in sequence — e.g., historical, moral, allegorical, and anagogical — to reinforce and clarify meaning)
21. Thematic (derivation of a central theme from a portion of Scripture)
22. Collective (use of Scripture to interpret Scripture — catenae collections, etc.)
23. Scholastic (use of material, formal, efficient, and final cause-structure; analysis by means of division, distinction, definition, argument, allegation; etc., etc.)
24. Pandectal (combination of the preceding 23 methods)

How does this impressive scheme compare with the traditional Roman Catholic hermeneutics of the medieval period? It should be obvious, first of all, that Sixtus is dependent upon medieval hermeneutics for much of what appears in his categories labeled "definitional" and "inventional." The literal-mystical and the historical-tropological-allegorical-anagogical distinctions had deep roots in the Middle Ages.[69] The universal-particular opposition was basic in scholastic philosophy, and the six "inventional" ap-- proaches had been in use among rhetoricians and homileticians.[70] The very coupling together of "quadrivial" elements under the general head "mathematical" shows a dependence upon the tri- vium-quadrivium structure of medieval education. Sixtus him- self in effect admits his lack of originality with regard to "defini- tional" and "inventional" interpretation, and says that he will concentrate chiefly upon the "methodical" approach, for "even to this day it has never been described or treated by any author."[71] Although even in the cast of "methodical" hermeneutic Sixtus is obviously dependent upon his predecessors (note especially method 23), he is quite correct in stating that no one before him had explicitly brought together such a detailed scheme for Biblical interpretation. Moreover, when Sixtus places strong em- phasis on the cabala in his treatment of the "elementive" approach in "definitional" hermeneutics, he shows that he is never a mere Roman traditionalist.[72] In comparison with medieval Biblical in-

[69] See Harry Caplan: "The Four Senses of Scriptural Interpretation and the Mediaeval Theory of Preaching," *Speculum,* IV (1929), 282-90. For readers unfamiliar with the traditional four-fold scheme, the following ex- ample should be helpful: "Guibert illustrates how to interpret the word 'Jerusalem.' Literally, it is the city of that name; allegorically, it represents Holy Church; tropologically, it signifies the faithful soul of whosoever as- pires to the vision of eternal peace; anagogically ['leading up' to the con- templation of heavenly things], it denotes the life of the dwellers in Heaven who see God revealed in Zion" (*ibid.,* p. 283).

[70] Cf. Harry Caplan: "Rhetorical Invention in Some Mediaeval Tractates on Preaching," *Speculum,* II (1927), 284-95.

[71] *Bibliotheca sancta,* p. 179.

[72] Cabalistic methods of interpretation were of course known, at least in some degree, to Christian scholars of the medieval period (Caplan, *Speculum,* IV, 289); however, Christian circles did not feel the real impact of the cabala until the Renaissance, when Pico of Mirandola had much to do with its popularization among Christians; see Joseph Leon Blau: *The Christian Interpretation of the Cabala in the Renaissance* (New York, 1944). We have already seen that Sixtus preserved two thousand cabalistic books from destruction at Cremona, and it is evident from his biographical sketch

terpretation, it can be said on the positive side that Sixtus reflects
the new scholarship of the Renaissance: he stresses the use of such
tools of Biblical scholarship as the polyglot Bible, whose importance had become evident through Cardinal Ximenes de Cisneros'
great Complutensian Polyglot; and although he gives a place to
traditional scholastic technique, his interests are by no means
circumscribed by the scholastic. On the negative side, his very
multiplying and distinguishing of methods is seen to be an extension — though perhaps an unconscious extension — of scholastic
atomism; moreover, in his attempt at Renaissance comprehensiveness and inclusiveness, Sixtus tends to lose perspective (as did
Pico of Mirandola) and to miss central motifs and devotional insights through a multiplicity of intellectualized methods.

As compared with Protestant Biblical interpretation of the sixteenth century, Sixtus' approach leaves much to be desired. It
is true that a constitutionally *unsystematischer* Luther might well
have benefited from the systematic techniques of the *Bibliotheca
sancta;* but if a choice has to be made between the radically Christ-
centered approach to the Bible on the part of the early reformers,
and the methodological scheme of Sixtus, the choice is not a
difficult one to make. The highly formal character of Sixtus'
method does not cut to the heart of Scripture, and his lack of
Luther's dynamic, central hermeneutic principle that "the whole
Scripture is about Christ alone everywhere"[73] gives an anthropocentric cast to his entire presentation. This last consideration
suggests what is perhaps the most potentially dangerous aspect
of Sixtus' entire approach: a tendency to stand *over* Scripture,

of Pico (*Bibliotheca sancta,* pp. 335-36) that he thought very highly of this
Christian cabalist. Sixtus devotes six pages to the cabala out of the fifteen
pages dealing with "definitional" interpretation; this high proportion is characteristic of a Renaissance, not a medieval, interpreter.

[73] Luther: *Vorlesung über den Römerbrief, 1515-16,* ed. J. Ficker (4th
ed.; Leipzig, 1930), p. 240. Cf. Watson, *op. cit.,* pp. 149-52, and Willem
Jan Kooiman: *Luther and the Bible,* tr. John Schmidt (Philadelphia, 1961),
passim. It is significant that Sixtus says nothing of such a principle in sections of his hermeneutic discussion which would seem to beg for it — e.g.,
in the "prophetic" subdivison of "definitional" interpretation, and in techniques 21 and 22 of "methodical" interpretation. Sixtus is far more inter-
ested in explaining the "46 years" in John 2:20 by noting that this is the
numerical cabalistic value of the Greek

A Δ AM (A=1, Δ=4, A=1, M=40; sum 46)!

and to control it by means of comprehensive techniques rather than to stand *under* it and allow the Christ of Scripture to control the interpreter. Obviously, there is nothing inherently presumptive in the use of technique, but when Sixtus speaks of his *methodi, seu viae, tractandis aptandisque sacrarum expositionum generibus idoneae*,[74] it is evident that he himself is thinking chiefly in terms of hermeneutic control of the sacred writings by the interpreter. And since his techniques are far more detailed than those of his medieval predecessors, the danger becomes proportionately greater.

Concluding Evaluation

If Sixtus of Siena was a true representative of Catholic Biblical scholarship in the Reformation period — and neither his contemporaries nor ours seem to doubt it — then one can derive from the foregoing discussion a picture both of the strengths and of the weaknesses of the Roman approach to the Scriptures during that epoch of conflict. On the one hand, Renaissance scholarship was brought to bear on the Biblical writings to an unprecedented degree, and the Renaissance ideal of comprehensiveness greatly influenced the Biblical interpreter. On the other hand, originality in Biblical scholarship tended to manifest itself in new and even more all-embracing scholasticisms, and the legalistic anthropocentrism which the Protestant reformers opposed with such vehemence became even more central in Roman Biblical herme-

---

[74] *Bibliotheca sancta*, p. 180; cf. the use of the term "absolutissima" in the title of Bk. 3 as separately published (see above, n. 57). Sixtus differs markedly from the reformers in this respect; indeed, the latter were even "antipathetic to the use of the four senses. Melanchthon regards it as the trifling and vicious recourse to a monstrous metamorphosis on the part of inept illiterates" (Caplan, *Speculum*, IV, 289). In contrast with Sixtus' rather stifling methodology, Johann Gerhard — as late as 1610 — gives only seven concise principles of Biblical interpretation in his mammoth *Loci theologici:* (1) Scripture is to be interpreted by Scripture; (2) Analogy of faith must be employed; (3) Clearer and more frequently reiterated passages should interpret more obscure and more isolated passages; (4) The original Hebrew and Greek texts are normative; (5) Scripture is to be understood literally unless non-literal interpretation is permitted by the Biblical passage itself; (6) Context and historical background of the text must be regarded; (7) Ancient and modern interpreters are to be utilized (I, 237-40).

neutics. If doctrinal formulations and Biblical interpretations are inextricably entwined through Christian history, it would be well for present-day students of the Protestant-Catholic dialogue to consider the implications of Sixtus' approach in the sixteenth-century dogmatic milieu. And Protestants especially might ponder the fact that Sixtus' *Bibliotheca sancta* was highly esteemed and constantly used by non-Catholics during the sixteenth and seventeenth centuries; it would seem more than likely that Sixtus played some small part in the Protestant *via dolorosa* from Christocentric Reformation through the scholasticism of later Orthodoxy to anthropocentric Enlightenment.

III

The Approach of New Shape Roman Catholicism to Scriptural Inerrancy: A Case Study for Evangelicals

III

The Approach of New Shape Roman Catholicism to Scriptural Inerrancy: A Case Study for Evangelicals*

gen. topic

At the beginning of each meeting of the Second Vatican Council, participants and observers witnessed an ancient oriental custom, newly reintroduced at the Council: the enthroning of the Book of the Gospels. This rite well symbolized the powerful Biblical revival in twentieth-century Roman Catholicism and reminded Protestants that Holy Scripture is not the private domain of the heirs of the Reformation. Indeed, Vatican II displayed at its very heart the concern for biblical understanding characteristic of Roman Catholic scholarship since the founding of the Ecole Biblique at Jerusalem by Père Marie-Joseph Lagrange;[1] as Jesuit R. A. F. MacKenzie has recently said of the Council's work: "Important as the Constitution on the Church is generally agreed to be, it is equaled in stature by the Constitution on Divine Revelation; the two are the most fundamental documents produced by the Second Vatican Council."[2] This laudable stress

* An invitational presentation at the Seminar on the Authority of Scripture (Harold John Ockenga, chairman), held at Gordon College, Wenham, Massachusetts, June 20-29, 1966.

[1] Cf. Montgomery, "The Fourth Gospel Yesterday and Today; An Analysis of Two Reformation and Two 20th-Century Commentaries on the Gospel According to St. John," *Concordia Theological Monthly*, XXXIV (April, 1963), 197-222 (containing an examination of Lagrange's *Evangile selon Saint Jean*).

[2] *The Documents of Vatican II*, ed. Walter M. Abbott (New York: Guild Press, America Press, Association Press, 1966), p. 107.

on the doctrine of revelation should goad contemporary Protestantism — too often preoccupied with achieving vaster ecclesiastical unions and non-theological goals — to re-examine its own biblical foundations. More particularly, the current Roman Catholic emphasis on revelation should receive the closest attention from evangelical Protestants who are endeavoring to clarify their historic position on the absolute authority, infallibility, and inerrancy of Holy Writ. It is the judgment of the present essayist that recent developments in Roman Catholic thinking on the revelational issue can provide an invaluable case study for evangelicals facing similar problems. No apology is offered for the negative thrust of later sections of the paper: I praise the Lord of the Church for all genuine enthronements of His scriptural Word, but I must also seek to distinguish what is truly honoring to His Word from what is not. And a valuable lesson can have a negative moral; as a very wise man once said, "Those who refuse to learn by history are forced to repeat its mistakes."

The Classical Roman Catholic Position on Biblical Inerrancy

Rome's position on the inspiration of Holy Scripture has, through the generations preceding our own, seemed exceedingly clear-cut and unambiguous both to her friends and to her enemies. The Council of Trent, though reacting strongly against the Reformation's formal principle of Sola Scriptura, stated in no uncertain terms the full inspiration of the Bible. In the Fourth Session of the Council (8 April 1546) a "Decree Concerning the Canonical Scriptures" was set forth, describing the Holy Writings as "vel oretenus a Christo, vel a Spiritu Sancto dictatas":

> The holy, ecumenical and general Council of Trent, lawfully assembled in the Holy Ghost, the same three legates of the Apostolic See presiding, keeps this constantly in view, namely, that the purity of the Gospel may be preserved in the Church after the errors have been removed. This [Gospel], of old promised through the Prophets in the Holy Scriptures, our Lord Jesus Christ, the Son of God, promulgated first with His own mouth, and then commanded it to be preached by His Apostles to every creature as the source at once of all saving truth and rules of conduct. It also clearly perceives that these truths and rules are contained in the written books and in the unwritten traditions, which, received by

the Apostles themselves, the Holy Ghost dictating, have come down to us, transmitted as it were from hand to hand. Following, then, the examples of the orthodox Fathers, it receives and venerates with a feeling of piety and reverence all the books both of the Old and of the New Testaments, since one God is the author of both, and also the traditions, whether they relate to faith or to morals, as having been dictated either orally by Christ or by the Holy Ghost, and preserved in the Catholic Church in unbroken succession.[3]

The subsequent centuries display the reinforcement of this strong biblical position over against heresies of various kinds.[4] Pius IX (1846-1878) condemned the pantheists, naturalists, and rationalists of his day for holding that "prophetiae et miracula in sacris Litteris exposita et narrata sunt poetarum commenta" and that "utriusque Testamenti libris mythica continentur inventa" (Denzinger, 1707). By the turn of the present century the Roman Church faced the Modernist controversy, and advocates (such as Loisy) of a partially inspired Scripture or of a Scripture erroneous in "non-theological" matters were condemned in no uncertain terms. In the Holy Office decree of 3 July 1907 ("Lamentabili"), Pius X (1903-1914) labeled as illegitimate the Modernist claim that "inspiratio divina non ita ad totam Scripturam sacram extenditur, ut omnes et singulas eius partes ab omni errore praemuniat" (Denzinger, 2011). Pius X's famous Encyclical "Pascendi dominici gregis" (8 September 1907) warrants extended quotation to show how firmly the Church rejected non-inerrancy views of Holy Writ:

The result of [the Modernist] dismembering of the records, and this partition of them throughout the centuries, is naturally that

---

[3] Denzinger, 783; *Canons and Decrees of the Council of Trent*, ed. H. J. Schroeder (St. Louis, Mo.: Herder, 1941), pp. 17, 296. It is not our purpose here to discuss the exact force of the word "dictatae"; surely it did not represent, even for Roman Catholics of the sixteenth century, a "mechanical" inspiration theory that cancelled out the personalities of the human authors of Scripture; but at the same time it leaves no room whatever for a biblical inspiration of limited or partial scope (cf. Montgomery, "Sixtus of Siena and Roman Catholic Biblical Scholarship in the Reformation Period," *Archiv fuer Reformationsgeschichte*, LIV/2 [1963], 214-34; reprinted in the present volume as Essay II).

[4] See the numerous documents collected in *Rome and the Study of Scripture*, ed. C. Louis (7th ed.; St. Meinrad, Indiana: Abbey Press, 1964).

the Scripture can no longer be attributed to the authors whose
names they bear. The Modernists have no hesitation in affirming
generally that these books, and especially the Pentateuch and the
first three Gospels, have been gradually formed from a primitive
brief narration, by additions, by interpolations of theological or allegorical interpretations, or by parts introduced only for the purpose
of joining different passages together. . . .

In the Sacred Books there are many passages referring to science
or history where, according to them, manifest errors are to be found.
But, they say, the subject of these books is not science or history,
but only religion and morals. In them history and science serve
only as a species of covering to enable the religious and moral ex-
periences wrapped up in them to penetrate more readily among
ancient people. The common people understood science and history
as they are expressed in these books, and it is clear that the expression of science and history in a more perfect form would have
proved not so much a help as a hindrance. Moreover, they add,
the Sacred Books, being essentially religious, are necessarily pul-
sating with life. Now life has its own truth and its own logic —
quite different from rational truth and logic, belonging as they do
to a different order, viz., the truth of adaptation and of proportion
to what they call its living medium and living purpose. Finally,
the Modernists, losing all sense of control, go so far as to proclaim
as true and legitimate whatever is explained by life.

We, Venerable Brethren, for whom there is but one and only
truth, and who hold that the Sacred Books, "written under the
inspiration of the Holy Ghost, have God for their author," [5] declare that this is equivalent to attributing to God Himself the lie
of expediency or the officious lie, and We say with St. Augustine:
"In an authority so high, admit but one officious lie, and there
will not remain a single passage of those apparently difficult to
practise or to believe, which on the same most pernicious rule may
not be explained as a lie uttered by the author willfully and to
serve some higher end." [6] And thus it will come about, the holy
Doctor continues, that "everybody will believe and refuse to believe what he likes or dislikes in them," namely, the Scriptures.
. . . In short, to maintain and defend these theories they [the
Modernists] do not hesitate to declare that the noblest homage

[5] Here Pius X quotes the "Constitutio dogmatica de fide catholicae,"
c. 2 ("De revelatione"), approved at Session III of Vatican I (24 April
1870), which in turn cites the Tridentine decree quoted earlier; see Denzinger, 1787.

[6] Augustine, Epist. 28, c. 3, in Migne's *Patrologiae cursus completus . . .
series latina*, XXXIII (August. ii), 112, 3.

that can be paid to the Infinite is to make it the object of contradictory statements! But when they justify even contradictions, what is it that they will refuse to justify? [7]

Loisy was excommunicated, and Pius X's successor, Benedict XV (1914-1922), underscored the inerrancy position of "Pascendi gregis" in his Encyclical "Spiritus Paraclitus" (15 September 1920).[8] To all intents and purposes, the partial and limited inspiration views of Catholic Modernism had been dealt the death blow. In point of fact, as George Lindbeck of Yale has correctly noted, Modernism went underground in the Roman communion, only to surface decades later after men sympathetic to a more radical biblical approach had attained positions of authority and influence in the Church.[9]

Biblical Criticism in New Shape Roman Catholic Scholarship

With the classic Roman Catholic stance on inerrancy before us, let us now observe the way in which representative scholars of that Church are presently approaching Holy Writ. The contrast will be instructive.

In 1958, Belgian Jesuit Jean Levie published a work which offers a synoptic view of the New Shape in Roman Catholic biblical scholarship. Its original title is significant (*La Bible, parole humaine et message de Dieu*)[10] for, unlike the title of the 1961 English translation (*The Bible, Word of God in Words of Men*), it well represents its author's major stress: the human rather than the divine aspects of the biblical writings. The book has two major sections, an overview of what Levie calls "progress in history and biblical exegesis" in recent Roman Catholicism, and a hermeneutic examination of Scripture problems, most of which display for him "the human traits in the inspired book." Here are some of his representative conclusions:

---

[7] Denzinger, 2100, 2102.
[8] *Ibid.*, 2186-2188.
[9] So Lindbeck, an official observer at Vatican II, stated in a course of lectures on contemporary Roman Catholic theology which he delivered at the Chicago Lutheran Theological Seminary (Maywood, Illinois) during the summer of 1961.
[10] Paris-Louvain: Desclée de Brouwer, 1958.

Scientific ideas current in those [biblical] days, but which have now been abandoned, may enter into the formulation of teaching which alone the inspired writer wishes to assert. It is, moreover, of little consequence whether he did or did not believe in the ideas current in his time, for they are not what he is claiming to assert.[11] It has been possible to discover in the Pentateuch a certain number of doublets — two accounts of the same events, but derived from different sources. There are divergencies in these accounts, since the two traditions are themselves divergent, but they have been combined in a single text by the inspired writer. . . . In J, the deluge lasts for forty days and Noe then opens the window to release the birds (8.6) and fourteen days later, he leaves the ark. In P, the period between the beginning of the Flood to the exit from the ark lasts for more than a year (7. 11 and 8. 14).[12]

There may be [in Scripture] fictional historical forms. . . . books which though apparently historical in form, seem in fact to be didactic writings, philosophical and religious discussions or theses.[13] In the last days of Judaism, we meet a special literary form, the . . . Haggadic Midrash. . . . It often became a list of marvels full of extraordinary or even fantastic events. . . . The hypothesis of an "inspired Haggadah" here and there (that is, an existing literary form used, under the inspiration of the Holy Spirit, for nobler ends), should not be necessarily excluded *a priori* by Catholic exegesis.[14]

Every nation writes the history of ancient times with the help of ancestral traditions, accounts that are partly historical, partly poetical, which in their passage from one generation to another, gradually simplify the facts, group them around some more outstanding personality, and artificially link stories which are independent of one another. . . . It is easy to discover significant concrete examples of this literary form in many of the Pentateuch narratives, for instance in the story of the patriarchs (Gen. chapters 11-50), and to throw into relief their character as collective, popular accounts, as ancestral traditions. In fact it was the study of these accounts which gave rise to the earliest applications of *Formgeschichte* (with H. Gunkel).[15]

The perspective on biblical truth expressed in these quotations from Levie is shared by his British confrère R. A. F. MacKenzie,

[11] Levie, *The Bible, Word of God in Words of Men,* trans. S. H. Treman (New York: P. J. Kenedy, 1961), pp. 216-17.

[12] *Ibid.,* pp. 221-22.

[13] *Ibid.,* pp. 222, 225.

[14] *Ibid.,* pp. 226-27.

[15] *Ibid.,* pp. 228-29.

S.J., whose 1963 publication, *Faith and History in the Old Testament,* has acquired considerable popularity both in England and in the United States. In the author's summation of his key chapter on "The Problem of Myth and History," one reads:

> For them [the Israelite historians], what really happened was what God did, and the material phenomena on the level of sense perception could be freely heightened and colored in their accounts, the better to express the reality that lay behind them.
>
> But when they had no history and traditions of their own, namely, for the period preceding the call of Abraham, then they were of necessity driven to take their materials where they could find them, and that meant only in the tradition and mythology that had originated among other peoples.[16]

American Jesuit John L. McKenzie, the first Roman Catholic to hold a chair at the University of Chicago Divinity School, offers a more generalized account of the same view, employing the personalistic-existential imagery of Martin Buber:

> Surely there now ought to be little room for timidity and misunderstanding if we call Hebrew literature in some passages mythical, or wisdom discourses couched in mythopoeic patterns. Even if the rigorous ethics of scholarship do not clearly demand the adoption of this terminology, they do demand the recognition of Israel's community with the ancient Near East in patterns of thought and language. . . . The Hebrew intuition of the ineffable reality which revealed itself to man as the personal reality behind the succession of phenomena, the agent of the great cosmic event which we call creation, the reality from which all things came, in which they exist, and to which they must return, was not the creation of mythical form or of logical discourse, but a direct and personal experience of God as the "Thou" to whom the human "I" must respond. But they had no media through which they could enunciate the ineffable reality except the patterns of thought and speech which they inherited from their civilization.[17]

[16] R. A. F. MacKenzie, *Faith and History in the Old Testament* (New York: Macmillan, 1963), pp. 80-81. Even more extreme expressions of this viewpoint coupled with the judgment that "an excessive preoccupation with inerrancy can stultify exegesis" (p. 328), mark Spanish Jesuit Luis Alonso Schökel's *The Inspired Word; Scripture in the Light of Language and Literature,* trans. Francis Martin (New York: Herder, 1965); for my review see Chapter V of the present book.

[17] John L. McKenzie, *Myths and Realities: Studies in Biblical Theology* (Milwaukee: Bruce Publishing Co., 1963), p. 200. In line with his general

In a strictly analogous way, Roman Catholic scholars in the New Testament field have been re-evaluating their materials. Myles M. Bourke's paper on "The Literary Genus of Matthew 1-2" is characteristic; in a manner strongly reminiscent of Loisy, he uses the fact that the infancy narrative parallels in literary genre a haggadic commentary to dispense with the historicity of many details of the biblical account.[18] The door had been opened for such an orientation by the Encyclical *Divino afflante Spiritu* (1943), which, though it did not advocate a radical approach to Scripture, clearly allowed the use of the *formgeschichtliche Methode* and made it possible for Roman Catholic scholars to doubt, for example, that given biblical miracles occurred historically if their doubt stemmed from conviction that the miracles were included as literary devices to illustrate theological points. Indeed, Roger Aubert has stated that Catholic exegetes could theoretically on this basis remain in full fellowship with the Church while denying all biblical miracles but the Virgin Birth and the Resurrection.[19]

Thus we arrive at the most recent official Roman Catholic statements on the nature of Scripture: the 1964 Instruction of the Biblical Commission on the historical truth of the Gospels, and Vatican II's Constitution on Divine Revelation. The Biblical Commission implicitly countenances Gospel interpretation by literary forms — not excluding miracle stories and midrash — and allows for *Redaktionsgeschichte;* and in this connection the Instruction "speaks of 'truth' only, and does not specify it as 'his-

existential orientation, McKenzie, as banquet speaker at the 7th Annual Meeting of the American Society of Christian Ethics (Seabury-Western Theological Seminary, Evanston, Illinois, January 22, 1966) severely criticized the traditional code morality of his Church and claimed that the New Testament requires only the *agape* ethic of responsible, personal decision in the situational context.

[18] *Catholic Biblical Quarterly*, XXII (1960), 160-75.

[19] If it is argued that the Encyclical *Humani generis* (1950) seems to restrict the liberty permitted by *Divino afflante Spiritu*, one need only consider Jesuit Gustave Lambert's well-received interpretation that *Humani generis* does not function in this manner; this is likewise the conclusion of Count Begouen, the eminent French anthropologist (see James M. Connolly, *The Voices of France; a Survey of Contemporary Theology in France* [New York: Macmillan, 1961], pp. 189-90).

torical truth.' "[20] Vatican II, in its Dogmatic Constitution on Divine Revelation, affirms that "the books of Scripture must be acknowledged as teaching firmly, faithfully, and without error that truth which God wanted put into the sacred writings for the sake of our salvation."[21] Explains the commentator:

> An earlier draft of the Constitution had joined the adjective *salutaris* ("tending to salvation") to the word "truth." Another last-minute change substituted the phrase "for the sake of our salvation," to avoid seeming to limit the truth itself. The point remains the same. . . .
>
> The Bible was not written in order to teach the natural sciences, nor to give information on merely political history. It treats of these (and all other subjects) only insofar as they are involved in matters concerning salvation. It is only in this respect that the veracity of God and the inerrancy of the inspired writers are engaged. This is not a quantitative distinction. . . . It is formal, and applies to the whole text. The latter is authoritative and inerrant in what it affirms about the revelation of God and the history of salvation. According to the intentions of its authors, divine and human, it makes no other affirmations.[22]

That this interpretation of the Constitution is eminently just can be seen from the history of the schema on revelation. "It is no secret that the first draft of the schema *De fontibus revelationis* contained two paragraphs which incorporated the terminology of the *Monitum* of June, 1961, and leveled anathemas against those who would call in question the genuine historical and objective truth of the words and deeds of Jesus *prouti narrantur*. This was rejected along with the rest of the schema."[23] Conservatives had attempted, unsuccessfully, to stem the tide; a recent article describes their views in the following terms:

> There exists a numerous and fairly articulate group convinced that the four Gospels and the Acts of the Apostles are genuine and objectively accurate historical documents, which can be used as

[20] Joseph A. Fitzmyer, S.J. (ed.), *The Historical Truth of the Gospels (The 1964 Instruction of the Biblical Commission) with Commentary* (Glen Rock, N.J.: Paulist Press, 1964), p. 14; Fitzmyer's edition of the Instruction appeared first in *Theological Studies*, XXV (September, 1964), 386-408.

[21] *The Documents of Vatican II (op. cit.,* in note 2 above), p. 119.

[22] *Ibid.*

[23] Fitzmyer, *op. cit.,* p. 18, n. 19.

such legitimately in the science of apologetics. These individuals insist that they have reason to hold and to teach that these events set forth in these books took place in the very way in which they are described in these works. They hold that the words and the deeds attributed to Our Lord were actually uttered and performed by Him.[24]

Clearly this position (with its evident affinity to the biblical orientation of classic evangelical Protestantism) is no longer officially advocated or even required of the Roman Catholic theologian. New Shape Catholic biblical scholarship displays a very different alignment: with the historical-critical method which won the day among non-evangelical Protestant scholars during the Modernist era and which has continued as the operating methodology in those circles even to the post-Bultmannian present. Thus James R. Robinson, a leading figure in the Protestant "New Quest of the Historical Jesus," comments favorably on Bourke's midrash interpretation of Matthew 1-2:

> The main difference between Bourke and Renan on this point would seem to be that Renan lived at a time when this position was inadmissible within the Roman Catholic Church and Bourke is living in a time when it is admissible. Form criticism has made it possible for the Catholic scholar to assert that the literal sense of a given passage is not to present a true story but rather a story conveying truth.[25]

In the same vein, Robinson approvingly cites Raymond E. Brown's dissertation, *The Sensus Plenior of Sacred Scripture* (1955), which in the last decade has shifted the attention of Roman Catholic exegetes from the *sensus literalis* to a "fuller sense" allegedly conveyed by the biblical text:

> The interest in *sensus plenior* has some affinities with Gerhard von Rad's interest in the successive reinterpretation of the Old Testament *Heilsgeschichte* within the successive oral and written layers of the Old Testament itself, or with Rudolf Bultmann's

[24] J. C. Fenton, "Father Moran's Prediction," *American Ecclesiastical Review*, CXLVI (1962), 194-95.

[25] James M. Robinson, "Interpretation of Scripture in Biblical Studies Today," in *Ecumenical Dialogue at Harvard: The Roman Catholic-Protestant Colloquium*, ed. Samuel H. Miller and G. Ernest Wright (Cambridge, Mass.: Belknap Press of Harvard University Press, 1964), p. 102.

detection that the Christology implicit in Jesus' mission becomes explicit in the Christological titles attributed to him after Easter.[26]

From Trent and Pius X to von Rad and Bultmann is a leap of staggering proportions. Let us now attempt to understand how it happened and to draw forth its implications for a contemporary evangelical theology of the Word.

The Rationale of Revolution

The historian can easily remind us of shifts in the twentieth-century theological climate which make the Roman Catholic acceptance of radical biblical scholarship seem more understandable. For example, by the 1940's when *Divino afflante Spiritu* was promulgated, the less theologically radical Protestant Neo-Orthodoxy had sufficiently replaced Protestant Modernism that a more liberal approach to the Bible no longer appeared to pose any direct threat to the Church. But such considerations only scratch the surface of a revolution so radical that, without any change of traditional terminology ("inerrancy," "dictation by the Holy Ghost," etc.) a Church which once set itself unequivocally against literary dismembering of biblical books and against errors of any kind in their inspired contents, now allows these very positions to be held by her scholars.

Protestants are frequently bewildered by such changes in the face of the supposedly unchanging Rome. Not too many years ago a Roman Catholic priest in Boston was excommunicated for maintaining strictly the medieval position, hallowed by a famous bull of Boniface VIII, that salvation absolutely necessitates submission to the Roman pontiff; in holding that non-Catholics would not be saved, the priest violated the conviction of present-day Catholic theology that non-Catholics will be judged by the "natural law" known to them. The priest in question was bewildered; but even more so were Protestants who observed what

[26] *Ibid.*, p. 105. Cf. the Protestant and Roman Catholic contributions to *Scripture and Ecumenism: Protestant, Catholic, Orthodox and Jewish,* ed. Leonard J. Swidler ("Duquesne Studies. Theological Series," 3; Pittsburgh, Pa.: Duquesne University Press, 1965).

appeared to be a blatant inconsistency in a Church claiming to be utterly consistent.

More recently, Father Hans Küng of Tübingen University electrified the theological world with his book, *Justification: The Doctrine of Karl Barth and a Catholic Reflection,* in which he argues in all seriousness that the Canons and Decrees of Trent, which were written in large part as an answer to the Reformer's central principle of Sola Gratia, are fully compatible with Barth's exposition of the historic Protestant doctrine of justification. Barth, in his Preface to Küng's book, wryly comments:

> All I can say is this: If what you have presented in Part Two of this book is actually the teaching of the Roman Catholic Church, then I must certainly admit that my view of justification agrees with the Roman Catholic view; if only for the reason that the Roman Catholic teaching would then be most strikingly in accord with mine! Of course, the problem is whether what you have presented here really represents the teaching of your Church.[27]

Here Barth betrays his Protestant mind-set: he questions whether Küng's reinterpretation of Trent can be squared with "the teaching" of the Roman Church. This is how a Protestant operates, to be sure; he assumes a permanent and perspicuous revelatory teaching in Holy Scripture, and then evaluates current theological interpretations against that standard. But this is not the way Rome does business theologically. Küng's activity looks bizarre to a Protestant, and *is* bizarre from the standpoint of Protestant theological methodology; but, when viewed from within the Roman Catholic understanding of theological truth, Küng's work is, in principle (wholly apart from the question of scholarly soundness), quite legitimate.

Rome's ultimate standard of religious truth is Rome itself: and by "Rome" is not meant a static body of historical creeds which impose their objective authority upon later generations, but rather a living organism which, as the extension of Christ's incarnation in time and as the vehicle of God's Holy Spirit, can creatively

[27] Barth, "A Letter to the Author," in Küng's *Justification,* trans. Collins, Tolk, and Granskon (New York: Thomas Nelson, 1964), p. xx. For my review of Küng's book, see Chapter V of the present volume.

reshape its past. Listen to one of the greatest modern exponents of "the spirit of Catholicism," Karl Adam:

> In reality Christianity is an intimate organic unity, a vital unity, which unfolds itself indeed to its fulness progressively, and yet in all the stages of its unfolding is a unity and a whole, the Christianity of Christ. Just as I first appreciate the totality of that potential life which is in the acorn when I see before me the mature oak, fully developed in all its grandeur, in a way that no mere study of the embryology of the acorn can enable me to realize it, so can I first discern the width and depth of Christ's Gospel, the whole vast richness of His mind and His message, His "fulness," when I have before me the fully-developed Christianity, and then only in the measure in which I appreciate its inner unity. . . . So there is in Catholic Christianity a unitary lifestream, a life of unity in fulness, a single mighty life. And if I would determine the content of the original cell of this life, the content of the Christianity of Christ, I must not approach the tree of Christianity with the knife of the critic and mutilate it in order to discover this original cell. On the contrary I must accept the Christian life as a whole and appraise it as a whole. Unlimited criticism, faulty and sterile historical or philological research: these things do not conduct us to the mystery of Christ. But we attain to Him by steeping ourselves lovingly in the abundance of life which has gone forth from Him.[28]

Once one understands the organic conception of truth at the heart of the Roman Church, one can see how ill-conceived was the excitement of many Protestant theologians and Vatican II observers when the Council did not incorporate into its Constitution on Divine Revelation the "two-source" theory (revelation is contained partly — *partim* — in Scripture and partly in the traditions) but stressed the unity of revelation: *Sola Scriptura in ore ecclesiae*. In point of fact, however one defines the source of revelation, the living Magisterium of the Church is the dynamic interpreter of it, shaping the Church's belief from age to age. Thus Adam describes the relation between Scripture and Magisterium:

> Christianity is not a religion of dead documents and fragmentary records, but a life in the Holy Spirit preserved from generation to

[28] Karl Adam, *The Spirit of Catholicism*, trans. Justin McCann (rev. ed.; Garden City, N.Y.: Doubleday Image Books, 1954), pp. 62-63.

generation by the apostolical succession of commissioned preachers
. . . The surging life of the Christian present flows over the dead
records of primitive documents, or rather, these documents are
themselves nothing but that life grown stiff and numb, nothing but
a deposit of that holy and supernatural life which still enfolds us
in the present. Therefore those documents can be fully deciphered
and yield their true revealed sense only in the light of this life.[29]

In precisely the same vein, R. A. F. MacKenzie summarizes the
viewpoint of Vatican II's Constitution on Divine Revelation:

A written record is a dead letter, needing constant interpretation
and commentary in succeeding ages. It cannot of itself answer new
questions, or explain what was once clear and has now become
obscure. But the writings transmitted in a living community, from
one generation to another, are accompanied by a continuous tradition of understanding and explanation which preserves and re-
expresses their meaning, and which applies them, from time to
time, to the solving of new problems. If this tradition were only
human, it would be liable to grave error. But such a consequence
is avoided by the Church's magisterium.[30]

This approach to the foundational documents of the Roman
Church (the Holy Scriptures) is of course applied to the subsequent documentary history of that body: all of its past records
are subject to perennial "decipherment" and "re-expression" by
the living Magisterium. Thus the about-face on *Extra ecclesiam
nullus salus;* thus the possibility of a re-reading of Trent in terms
of Sola Gratia; and thus the totally new understanding of biblical
inerrancy.

It is vital to note that from the Roman Catholic viewpoint, no
changes in doctrine actually take place in such cases. Once the
Magisterium reinterprets a teaching (e.g., the meaning of biblical
authority), then all previous authoritative expressions of the teaching are held to have this meaning. The powerful role of casuistry
in Roman Catholic moral theology parallels and encourages the
casuistical re-expression of documentary meaning in the Church's
dogmatic theology. To the non-Catholic, this procedure invariably suggests the Marxist rewriting of history and George Orwell's apocalyptic novel, *1984,* where Winston, the hapless vic-

---

[29] *Ibid.,* p. 232.
[30] *The Documents of Vatican II (op. cit.* in note 2 above), p. 109.

tim of a totalitarianism so complete that it continually rede
truth, searches in vain for a way to convince his persec
O'Brien, that the state has fallen into the worst epistemolo
hell of all, solipsism.[31]

Whether or not Roman Catholicism's organic view of theological truth amounts to solipsism is too large a question for us
to answer here.[32] But we do need to see that in its re-interpreta-
tion of the concept of biblical inspiration and inerrancy, the
Church has in fact sapped all significant meaning out of these
doctrines. Any assertion — religious or otherwise — which is compatible with anything and everything says precisely nothing.[33]
If I claim that my wife is an excellent driver, and yet cheerfully
admit that she has a serious accident weekly which is invariably
her fault, then my original claim (though I may continue to voice
it) is nonsense. By the same token, when Roman Catholicism
continues to insist that the Holy Scriptures were dictated by the
Holy Ghost and are inerrant, while at the same time allowing
internal contradictions through source conflation, external contradictions with known fact, employment of Midrash fictions, etc.,
the Church speaks nonsense. The argument that Scripture is in
any case inerrant *theologically* is of no help at all, since the biblical writers make no distinction whatever between "theological"
and "secular" fact, and indeed ground heavenly truth in earthly
reality ("If I have told you earthly things, and ye believe not,
how shall ye believe, if I tell you of heavenly things?" — John
3:12).[34] And the redefinition of biblical truthfulness in per-

31 On Marxist historiography and Orwell's *1984*, see Montgomery, *The Shape of the Past: An Introduction to Philosophical Historiography* ("History in Christian Perspective," Vol. 1; Ann Arbor, Mich.: Edwards Brothers, 1963), pp. 8-9, 74-75, 80-81, 217-56, 275-77.

32For further discussion on the subject, see my article, "Evangelical Unity in the Light of Contemporary Orthodox Eastern-Roman Catholic-Protestant Ecumenicity," *The Springfielder*, XXX (Autumn, 1965), 8-30 (published in shorter form under the title, "Evangelical Unity and Contemporary Ecumenicity," in *The Gordon Review*, IX [Winter, 1966], 69-90, and reprinted in the present volume as Essay I).

33 Cf. Montgomery, *The 'Is-God-Dead?' Controversy* (Grand Rapids, Mich.: Zondervan, 1966), *passim*.

34 I have developed this point at some length in my article, "Inspiration and Inerrancy: A New Departure," *Evangelical Theological Society Bulletin*,

sonalistic, existential categories ("I-Thou") by such Roman Catholic writers as John L. McKenzie only begs the question, for
"encounters" are not self-authenticating,[35] and the Scripture itself makes truth-as-encounter dependent upon truth-as-factual reality ("If I do not the works of my Father, believe me not" —
John 10:37). In New Shape Roman Catholic biblical theology,
the words "authority," "infallibility," and "inerrancy" have been
suffering what R. M. Hare has called the "death by a thousand
qualifications": they have been qualified again and again — to
such a point that they mean little or nothing. This is particularly
evident from the fact that Roman Catholic biblical scholars now
accept many of the radically critical arguments espoused by Protestant exegetes such as von Rad and Bultmann, who use these
very arguments to support their *rejection* of theopneustic biblical
authority.

To be sure, for Roman Catholics this problem is not particularly acute. The final authority is the living Magisterium, which,
a priori, stands above criticism. Words, documents, and entire
epochs of Church history have suffered the death of a thousand
qualifications, and Rome still remains; ever-changing, ever the
same. But what about the Protestant evangelical who, without
a Magisterium, contemplates the path taken by his Roman
Catholic counterpart?

The Evangelical Sine Qua Non: Biblical Authority Defined Hermeneutically

In some quarters today, evangelical Protestants are apparently
of the opinion that, like the Church of Rome, they can use the
general terminology of biblical authority ("infallibility," "in-

VIII (Spring, 1965), 45-75; this essay appears in revised form in my book,
Crisis in Lutheran Theology (2 vols.; Grand Rapids, Mich.: Baker Book
House, 1967), I, 15-44.

[35] See Frederick Ferré, *Language, Logic and God* (New York: Harper,
1961), chap. viii ("The Logic of Encounter"), pp. 94-104; C. B. Martin,
"A Religious Way of Knowing," in *New Essays in Philosophical Theology*,
ed. Antony Flew and Alasdair Macintyre (London: SCM Press, 1955),
pp. 76-95; and Kai Nielsen, "Can Faith Validate God-Talk?" in *New Theology No. 1*, ed. Martin E. Marty and Dean G. Peerman (New York: Macmillan Paperbacks, 1964).

errancy," and the like) without committing themselves to a view of biblical truthfulness in the particulars. Thus a rece news item reported: "Canadian representatives of the Missou.. Synod, The American Lutheran Church, and the Lutheran Church in America have agreed that a 'discrepancy' or an 'error of fact' can't affect the inerrancy of the Bible, according to a Canadian Lutheran Council report."[36] To which the present essayist replied:

> Whenever we reach the point of affirming on the one hand that the Bible is infallible or inerrant and admitting on the other hand to internal contradictions or factual inaccuracies within it, we not only make a farce of language, promoting ambiguity, confusion, and perhaps even deception in the church; more reprehensible than even these things, we in fact deny the plenary inspiration and authority of Scripture, regardless of the theological formulae we may insist on retaining. . . . I must — if only on the basis of common sense — protest the idea that "error can't affect inerrancy." This is like saying that the presence of corners can't affect a circle.[37]

My strong reply was an effort to remind my fellow churchmen of the centrality of unqualified biblical authority in their heritage. The Reformation irrevocably stated its theological claims upon a totally reliable, perspicuous Bible; it explicitly denied the notion of a living Magisterium as interpreter of Scripture. Indeed, the Reformers categorically refused to allow any human writing or teacher to stand above Holy Writ; they recognized full well that if God's Word were not entirely trustworthy, then man would be forever incapable of distinguishing its truth from its non-truth and even the salvatory Gospel would be imperiled.

During the heyday of Protestant Modernism, evangelicals were especially sensitive to the erosion of theological vocabulary among their Liberal opponents. They were well aware that

---

[36] *Lutheran Witness Reporter: Great Lakes Edition*, May 8, 1966, p. 1.

[37] *Lutheran Witness Reporter: Great Lakes Edition*, May 22, 1966, p. 7. Cf. Montgomery, "Lutheran Hermeneutics and Hermeneutics Today," in *Aspects of Biblical Hermeneutics* ("Concordia Theological Monthly. Occasional Papers," No. 1; St. Louis, Mo., 1966), pp. 78-108 (reprinted in *Crisis in Lutheran Theology* [op. cit.], I, 45-77).

without an infallible Magisterium the redefinition of terms such as "atonement" and "miracle" through pressure from the non-revelatory human situation would cause the Gospel — the material principle of the Reformation — to die the death of a thousand qualifications. Now, I submit, the same danger faces the formal principle — Scriptural authority.

And how are we to avoid this deleterious state of affairs? By a realistic recognition that *our statements of biblical inspiration, whatever their terminology* — whether positive ("entire trustworthiness") or negative ("infallibility," "inerrancy") — *having been derived from the general pronouncements of Scripture itself on the subject and particularly from the attitude of Christ and His chosen Apostles toward Scripture, must yield concrete hermeneutic guidelines for treating specific exegetical difficulties.* A doctrine of inspiration imposed upon the Bible from without is a denial of inspiration; a doctrine of limited biblical authority derived from passages manifesting difficulties is as false an induction and as flagrant a denial of the analogy of Scripture as is a morally imperfect Christology derived from questionable acts on Jesus' part (in both cases, proper induction requires that we go to the express teaching on the subject and allow this to create the inductively-derived *Gestalt* or pattern for treating particular problems);[38] and any doctrine of biblical authority without express hermeneutic application is already in the throes of the death by a thousand qualifications.

Quite obviously it would go beyond the scope of this paper to set forth a full-orbed doctrine of biblical authority governed by these criteria. But some suggestions can and ought to be made. When one observes the teaching and example of Christ

[38] A non-biblical example may help here. In understanding modern stream-of-consciousness writing (e.g., portions of James Joyce's *A Portrait of the Artist As a Young Man;* his *Ulysses;* parts of Faulkner's *The Sound and the Fury;* Salinger's *Catcher in the Rye*), the reader is hopelessly led astray by the *indicia* until he discovers, through the express teaching of the novel, the actual age of the character involved. Having learned this, he has an inductively derived *Gestalt* for understanding the particulars of the stream-of-consciousness narration; to reverse the procedure would be to lose all hope of meaningful interpretation.

and His chosen Apostles[39] on the subject of scriptural authority,
one is overwhelmingly impressed by the attitude of *total trust*
involved; nowhere, in no particular, and on no subject is Scripture subjected to criticism. Passages are quoted authoritatively
from the most obscure corner of the Old Testament; individual
words are forced to bear the weight of heavy doctrinal teaching;
passages from diverse periods and from the pens of many authors are quoted together and sometimes conflated, obviously
implying their consistency and common Divine authorship; no
attempt is made to distinguish truth "in faith and practice" from
veracity in historical and secular matters; and we are told that
man lives ἐπὶ παντὶ ῥήματι ἐκπορευμένῳ διὰ στόματος θεοῦ.
(Matt. 4:4, quoting Deut. 8:3).

A scripturally grounded doctrine of biblical authority thus
implicates (in the strictest sense) an inerrant, non-contradictory
Bible, and qualitatively distinguishes Scripture from all extra-
biblical materials, such that none of them can be used to judge
or criticize Holy Writ. If it is objected that we are implicitly
importing a standard of consistency into our doctrine of scriptural authority, we can only reply that man is incapable of com-
prehending anything apart from the law of contradiction (as
Emerson said to Brahma, "When me they fly, I am the wings"),
so a "revelation" involving contradiction reveals nothing at all.
Moreover, from a contradiction anything follows, so that the
presence of any contradictions in God's Word would require
the immediate testing of all its alleged truths — an impossible
task in the very matters most vital to salvation. Thus the popular analogy breaks down between the Scripture and a sermon
("Can't a sermon reveal truth even with mistakes in it?"): the
only way one knows that a sermon *does* reveal truth is by comparison of its teachings with Scripture; but there is no Bible-to-
the-second-power by which to test the veracity of the *Bible's*

[39] Christ gave His Apostles a special gift of the Holy Spirit which we
today would probably term "total recall" (see John 14:26-27; 16:12-15;
cf. Acts 1:21-26); this is the basis of the scriptural authority of the New
Testament writings, which were produced in Apostolic circles. On this and
the status of Paul as an Apostle, see my *Shape of the Past* (*op. cit.* in note
31 above), pp. 138-39, 171-72.

salvatory teachings. And (to repeat the warning Jesus gave to Nicodemus when He preached the Gospel to him): "If I have told you earthly things, and ye believe not, how shall ye believe, if I tell you of heavenly things?"

In conclusion, then, let us set forth the basic hermeneutic implications of this evangelical view of biblical authority, thereby preserving it from the death of a thousand qualifications to which New Shape Roman Catholic inspiration doctrine is unhappily subject. Though other hermeneutic guidelines could doubtless be added, the following six principles should make clear the over-all interpretive implications of biblical authority for our day:

1. A passage of Holy Writ must be taken as veracious in its natural sense (*sensus literalis*) unless the context of the passage itself dictates otherwise, or unless an article of faith established elsewhere in Scripture requires a broader understanding of the text.
2. The prime article of faith applicable to the hermeneutic task is the attitude of Christ and His Apostles toward the Scriptures: their utter trust in Scripture — in all it teaches or touches — must govern the exegete's practice, thus eliminating in principle any interpretation which sees the biblical texts as erroneous or contradictory in fulfilling their natural intent.
3. Harmonization of scriptural difficulties should be pursued within reasonable limits, and when harmonization would pass beyond such bounds, the exegete must leave the problem open rather than, by assuming surd error, impugn the absolute truthfulness of the God who inspires all Holy Scripture for our learning.
4. Extra-biblical linguistic and cultural considerations must be employed ministerially, never magisterially, in the interpretation of a text; and any use of extra-biblical material to arrive at an interpretation inconsistent with the veracity of the scriptural passage is to be regarded as magisterial and therefore illegitimate. Extra-biblical data can and should put questions to a text, but only Scripture itself can in the last analysis legitimately answer questions about itself.
5. Not all literary forms are consistent with scriptural revelation; the exegete must not appeal to literary forms (such as the midrash) which cast doubt on the truthfulness or the morality of the Divine author of Scripture.[40]

[40] A point well made by Augustin Cardinal Bea in his valuable syllabus, *De inspiratione et inerrantia Sacrae Scripturae; notae historicae et dogmaticae quas in usum privatum auditorum composuit* (new ed.; Rome: Pontificium Institutum Biblicum, 1954), pp. 44-45, but unfortunately ignored by most

6. The exegete should employ all scholarly research tools that do not involve rationalistic commitments. Rationalistic methodologies are identifiable by their presuppositions, which either (like Bultmann's demythologizing) do violence to articles of faith, or (like certain documentary theories) oppose the perspicuity of the received biblical texts and the facticity of the events recorded in them, or (like the "circularity principle" of the so-called "New Hermeneutic") give to the sinful cultural milieu, past and present, a constitutive role in the formulation of biblical teaching.[41] These and other rationalistic techniques are to be scrupulously avoided in carrying out the hermeneutic task.

But to conclude an essay on the perfection of Scripture with less than the perfect number of principles seems woefully inappropriate; and to terminate an essay focusing on the Roman Church without quoting one of her greatest saints would be indeed ungracious. So let us hear again from St. Augustine, who will provide our seventh and foundational principle for the reading of that Sacred Book which brought him, and by God's grace brings each of us, into the presence of the saving Christ:

7. In an authority so high, admit but one officious lie, and there will not remain a single passage of those apparently difficult to practise or to believe, which on the same most pernicious rule may not be explained as a lie uttered by the author willfully and to serve some higher end.[42]

representatives of New Shape Roman Catholic biblical scholarship. See also Bea's excellent work, *The Study of The Synoptic Gospels; New Approaches and Outlooks,* ed. Joseph A. Fitzmyer (New York: Harper, 1965).

[41] On the incompatibility between the "New Hermeneutic" (represented by Ebeling, Fuchs, Ott, Conzelmann, G. Bornkamm, *et al.*) and the hermeneutic of the Reformation, see my essay, "Lutheran Hermeneutics and Hermeneutics Today" (cited above in note 37).

[42] See above, note 6 and corresponding text.

IV

Rome and the "Death of God"

IV

Rome and the "Death of God"

The death-of-God movement displays less and less vitality with each passing month. It would seem that this quasi-religious phenomenon, centering as it does on the motif of mortality, is itself experiencing death-throes.

An oblique indicator the the cry "God is dead" is losing its force is the appearance of an anthology of "Readings in the Death of God Theology" (*Toward a New Christianity,* edited by Thomas J. J. Altizer). This volume—though it conveniently omits bibliographic reference to *The Altizer-Montgomery Dialogue* (Inter-Varsity Press), which certainly marks at least one step in the decline of theothanatology — suggests that this "radical" movement has already reached the unenviable bourgeois stage of collected "readings."

But an even more direct evidence that death-of-God is dying was provided last June 21 (1967), when Professor Altizer addressed a philosophy workshop at The Catholic University of America on "The Problem of God in Contemporary Thought." Having found his position roundly rejected by virtually all strata of Protestant thought, Altizer emphatically stated that if there proves to be no possibility that Roman Catholic theology will move in the direction of his "totally christocentric" form of faith and the dialectical self-negation of God, then "I for one will be reluctantly forced to concede that an atheistic or death of God theology is a destructive aberration." Quite a concession!

What has convinced Altizer that he should now put all his atheological eggs in a Roman Catholic basket? The answer is not hard to find, and it is an exceedingly instructive one for those Christians now celebrating the 450th anniversary of the Reformation.

Let us begin by recalling the essence of Altizer's position: his affirmation of God's death is a variant of archaic nineteenth century Hegelianism. He begins by rejecting the law of non-contradiction (on which all logical thinking is based) and substitutes for it Hegel's so-called "dialectic logic" of perpetual thesis, antithesis, and synthesis, whereby religious truth undergoes self-negation and thus progressively rises to higher and higher levels, issuing out in a "God beyond God" and a "fully kenotic Word." This totally hidden Christ (which must not be "identified with the original historical Jesus") is encountered in the secular, profane present and even more fully in the apocalyptic "third age of the Spirit" growing in the crucible of today's secularism. (See my *The 'Is God Dead?' Controversy* [Zondervan] and my chapter in Bernard Murchland's *The Meaning of the Death of God* [Random House].)

At Catholic University Altizer effortlessly related these views to contemporary thinking in the Roman church. In contrast to historic Protestantism, which relies on the Bible as God's sole and final revelation of truth, the modern Catholic thinker — whose greatest model is provided by the evolutionary theology of Teilhard de Chardin — conceives of a dynamic or evolving Christ. This Christ is progressively manifested in the growth of his Body, the Church — an organic development inseparable from the total body of humanity. "Once we are liberated from the root idea that the biblical and apostolic images of God have an absolute and eternal authority, then" — Altizer underscored the lesson for modern Catholics — "we can become open to the possibility that everything which orthodox Christianity has known as God is but a particular stage of God's self-manifestation, and must in turn be transcended by the forward movement of God Himself."

Doubtless Altizer goes too far in his endeavor to create a one-to-one correlation between Rome's world-view and process-thought. Aristotelian logic, St. Thomas' passion for objective, final truth, and the respect given through the centuries to the inerrant Scriptures and creedal verities are too much a part of Rome's life to be brushed lightly aside. But Altizer is not mistaken when he points up the extent to which evolutionary, process thinking influences the contemporary Catholic mind.

Karl Adam, in his classic *The Spirit of Catholicism*, argued that true Catholic Christianity must not be seen in the "embryonic" state (its original biblical documents) but rather in its "progressive unfolding," even as the oak must be seen not as an acorn but in its full maturity. Today many Catholics regard their church as a living organism that, as the extension of Christ's incarnation, can creatively reshape its past: "reinterpreting" past pronouncements such as *extra ecclesiam nulla salus* ("outside the Church there is no salvation") so as to give them totally new force. Once the Magisterium does reinterpret a past teaching, then all previous authoritative expressions of the teaching are held to carry this meaning: the past is rewritten in terms of the dynamic, living present. (See my paper, "The Approach of New Shape Roman Catholicism to Scriptural Inerrancy," which appears as Essay III in the present volume.)

To the Reformation Protestant, this procedure invariably suggests both the Marxist (*dialectic*, note well) rewriting of history and George Orwell's *1984*, where Winston, the citizen of a totalitarian world in which truth is continually "evolved" and "redefined," comes to realize that his society has fallen into the epistemological hell of solipsism. The Protestant knows well — or ought to know well — that unless an objective Word from God stands over against the Church, judging it and proclaiming grace to it, the Church invariably deifies itself, thereby engaging in the worst kind of idolatry. When any corporate body lacking a clear external standard of truth grows in strength, it strives to become a standard to itself, a law to itself: a Leviathan, the "mortal god" described by Hobbes. Solovyov, in his *Short Story of Antichrist* (*Christianity Today*, Jan. 2, 1965), well showed that where objective revelational truth ceases to provide a firm criterion of action, no church has the holiness to withstand the blandishments of antichristic power. (Cf. my essay, "Evangelical Unity and Contemporary Ecumenicity," which serves as Chapter I in the present work.)

From all sides today efforts are being made to unite Christendom ecumenically on the basis of vague dreams of evolving, process truth (a particularly unfortunate example being the writings of Charles J. Curtis, who employs Söderblom as a bridge to join Protestant with Catholic à la Whiteheadian process-thought). Altizer delineated the issue precisely when he asserted at Catholic University: "Any genuine evolutionary understanding of God is incompatible with the idea of an original deposit of faith which is absolute and given or unchanging."

Here is the watershed: *Was* God in Christ, objectively reconciling the world unto himself? *Did* he "once in the end of the world [appear] to put away sin by the sacrifice of himself" (Heb. 9:26)? *Has* God spoken with absolute finality in the Holy Scriptures, which testify of Christ? If so, process-theology in all its forms must receive the kiss of death. For only the Christ of Scripture, who is the same yesterday, today, and forever, can offer Church and society a genuine Resurrection and Life.

V

Three Reviews

V

Three Reviews

*Hans Küng on Justification — Alonzo Schökel on Holy
Scripture — Archbishop Söderblom's Ecumenicity*

1. Hans Küng on Justification

Justification: The Doctrine of Karl Barth and a Catholic Reflection by Hans Küng. Thomas Nelson, 1964. 332 pp.

Can Roman Catholics accept the cardinal Protestant doctrine of justification by grace alone through faith? One of the most explosive theologians of Rome's "New Shape" — the 39-year-old theological dean of Tuebingen and an active contributor to Vatican II — here answers with an emphatic "Yes" a question which could not even have been posed twenty years ago.

Küng, whose controversial writings made him *persona non grata* at ultraconservative Catholic University of America in 1963, endeavors to demonstrate the amazing thesis that the Tridentine decrees are completely hospitable to Protestant *sola fide* as displayed in Barth's *Church Dogmatics*. Barth, in an illuminating prefatory letter, can only say that Küng has accurately presented his (Barth's) theology, though he doubts whether Küng has done justice to his own (Roman) church teaching!

But an even more telling criticism is demanded. Küng, like other *aggiornamento* theologians, too readily assumes contemporary, neo-orthodoxy represents orthodox Reformation Protes-

103

tantism. This is, however, far from the case. Before evangelicals become too enthusiastic over Küng's efforts, they should read such works as Sasse's *Here We Stand,* Wingren's *Theology in Conflict,* Van Til's *Christianity and Barthianism* and Gordon Clark's *Karl Barth's Theological Method,* to discover the subtle relativizing of Reformation doctrine carried out by Barth.

2. *Alonzo Schökel on Holy Scripture*

The Inspired Word: Scripture in the Light of Language and Literature by Luis Alonzo Schökel. Translated by Francis Martin. Herder and Herder, 1965. 418 pp.

Most Protestants are aware of the revolutionary changes going on in the Roman Catholic Church today. Hardly a month passes but the general news magazines and the religious press feature striking alterations in Rome's ecclesiastical climate.

Protestants generally assume that the "New Shape" in Roman theology and practice is a good thing, since, quite obviously, the Rome of Pope John XXIII and Vatican II has drawn closer to scriptural practice in such matters as vernacular worship, tolerance of other Christians, the centrality of Christ, and encouragement of Bible reading. All these emphases are indeed worthy of highest commendation, but Jesuit Schökel's latest book points up a darker side of Rome's new posture.

Schökel, like R. A. F. MacKenzie (*Faith and History in the Old Testament*), John L. McKenzie (*Myths and Realities: Studies in Biblical Theology*), and Jean Levie (*La Bible, parole humaine et message de Dieu*), exemplifies a current tendency in Roman biblical study to fly from one extreme to the other. Fifty years ago Roman Catholic biblical scholarship was virtually a law unto itself, having little interest in the work of Bible students in other Christian communions.

Now the pendulum has swung to the other extreme, and many Roman Catholics are absorbing the prevailing mind-set of radical Protestant biblical interpreters. Two characteristics are especially prominent here, and they are both evident throughout Schökel's treatment of scriptural inspiration: an existentialist emphasis on "mystery" and "interpersonal knowledge," in contrast to the classic theological stress, from Augustine to Pius X, on the propositional truth of Scripture; and a de-emphasis on biblical inerrancy in favor of the allegedly diverse "literary forms" of scriptural address, which may or may not convey *de facto* truth.

Thus we are told that by regarding Scripture as "literary truth," we can see that "information is accidental": "the sacred author . . . can simplify the facts, he can accept the information without troubling to find out if it is completely exact, he can make up some of the information and use it in his work, he can distort things in the interest of narrative or expression, or he can exaggerate them."

Of course, for Roman Catholics the radical criticism of Holy Scripture can never touch the mainspring of religious authority, which is held to be the living Church itself. Schökel can therefore write: "The formula 'inspired books' is too vague and problematic. Inerrancy should be predicated of the Scriptures as they have been intrusted to the Church."

For the Protestant, however, such an approach to the Bible is suicidal, for if God's Word lacks total veracity, sinful man must himself judge that Word, thereby becoming his own god. But in fact God the Holy Spirit has spoken with clarity and utter truthfulness in the Sacred Scriptures, and man can only live "by every word that proceedeth out of the mouth of God."

3. Archbishop Söderblom's Ecumenicity

Söderblom: Ecumenical Pioneer by Charles J. Curtis. Augsburg, 1967. 149 pp. plus plates.

Faced with the remarkable diffuseness and variegated colors of today's ecumenical movement, how does one get one's bearings? Is there a key to discovering the central themes of modern ecumenicity? One of the surest ways is to investigate in depth the root concerns of an unquestioned leader of the 20th century thrust toward church union. Nathan Söderblom (1866-1931) eminently fills the bill, for he not only attained the highest ecclesiastical office in his own church (archbishop of Uppsala) but was instrumental in bringing about intercommunion between

Swedish Lutherans and the Church of England, and was the person most responsible for the success of the "Life and Work Movement," one of the two constituent elements in the formation of the World Council of Churches. In the absence of English translations of most of Söderblom's writings, it is useful to have a brief, readable, and up-to-date survey of his life and thought in book form.

But, as Gabriel Naudé well noted as far back as the 17th century (*Advice on Establishing a Library*), where many books are published on a subject, you can choose the best, but where few books are written, you will have to settle for what you can get. Were Söderblom widely treated in English, Curtis' book would have difficulty standing comparison. Why? Because the book engages in a very subtle special-pleading. Though Söderblom's theological failings are briefly touched on in the final chapter, they are softened as much as possible, and, set against the positive portrait drawn in the rest of the book, they appear to be little more than peccadillos — certainly not of sufficient importance to remove from Söderblom's genuine Lutheranism and sound ecumenical programs. Curtis actually states at the beginning of his critical section: "I myself consider the twelve criticisms to be either invalid, irrelevant, or too weakly argued" (p. 118). And earlier in the book the author asserts: "The ecumenical vision of the churches' movement toward unity is inconceivable for Söderblom without orthodoxy" (p. 102).

This statement is simply incredible — unless one redefines "orthodoxy" beyond all verbal significance. In point of fact, Söderblom's theology can hardly be considered Christian, to say nothing of Lutheran. In spite of his romantic attachment to Luther, the Archbishop played fast and loose with all of the life-and-death doctrines of the Protestant Reformation. In *The Nature of Revelation* (1903), he defended radical higher criticism of the Bible and claimed that revelation is restricted neither to the Scriptures (the Protestant view) nor to the Church (Catholicism) but continues in history throughout the ages. Here and elsewhere he showed direct dependence on Alfred Loisy, who was excommunicated by the Roman Church in 1908 for his modernism. Söderblom rejected the doctrine of the two natures of Christ as unacceptable to modern man, and in line with Ritschlian Liberalism he took religious experience (the idea of "holiness") as his theological point of departure instead of God-revealed doctrinal truth. From such religious vagaries to his ecumenical activities was but a short step: since biblical truth was not definitive, it could offer no serious barrier to the union of widely-divergent confessional bodies.

How does it happen that these considerations have so little influence in Curtis' book? The answer (which is nowhere explicitly spelled out in the work) is the author's own overriding theological viewpoint: Whiteheadian process-theology, inherited during LCA pastor Curtis' studies at the University of Chicago Divinity School. For the process-theologian, all doctrine and church practice must be redefined in "dynamic" rather than "static" terms: as Curtis said in conversation with the present reviewer on one occasion, "There are no absolutes." It is Curtis' hope that the process-motif, as displayed in Söderblom's concept of "continuing revelation," can provide the theme to unify Roman Catholicism (with its view of the Church as the continuing incarnation of Christ in time), mystical-existential Eastern Orthodoxy, and a Protestantism which no longer regards the biblical Word as an absolute. But as the pre-Socratic philosopher Heraclitus well recognized, "Out of flux nothing but flux comes." This ancient aphorism applies equally to modern ecumenical flux. The only hope for a true and solid ecumenicity is (contra Söderblom) a definitive Word from God revealing to us the nature of His truth and distinguishing that truth from error. With such a Word, ecumenical effort builds on rock; without it (and this is the tragedy of so much contemporary ecumenical activity) the result is sand, flux, and the general muddying of the Water of Life.

Index of Names